This book is dedicated to Justin, Ella, and Gavin. You inspire me every day to create healthy meals and share them with the world!

Table of Contents

Slow Cooking 101

Putting a healthy meal on the table each morning, each night, or at any time of the day is as easy as "Fixing-It and Forgetting-It!" Don't let being busy be the excuse anymore! Surround yourself with healthy ingredients and follow these easy and delicious recipes, and you'll have a healthy meal each and every time you put food on the table. You now have 150 healthy recipes in your hands. I honestly couldn't be more excited about sharing these wonderful recipes with you!

Let's talk about what makes this book so special . . .

This book is divided into six different categories for you: Breakfasts, Appetizers & Snacks, Soups, Stews & Chilies, Main Dishes, Side Dishes & Vegetables, and Desserts. Yes! You heard that right! There are even healthy desserts! Every recipe will be marked with symbols signaling if the recipe is Gluten-Free, Dairy-Free, Soy-Free, Nut-Free, Low-Cal, Low-Fat, Low-Sodium, Sugar-Free, Vegan, Vegetarian, Paleo, or High-Protein. For every recipe, we've included nutritional information to further help you with your dietary needs.

If you find a recipe you love, but it calls for an ingredient you can't have, please feel free to sub it with one that fits your particular allergen or dietary needs. For instance, if a recipe calls for peanut butter, but you have a peanut allergy, feel free to sub that for sunflower seed butter. Or, if a recipe calls for gluten-free soy sauce and you do not have a gluten-allergy or sensitivity, feel free to use regular soy sauce. Most of the recipes in this book can very easily be adjusted!

Choosing a Slow Cooker

Not all slow cookers are created equal . . . or work equally as well for everyone!

Those of us who use slow cookers frequently know we have our own preferences when it comes to which slow cooker we choose to use. For instance, I love my programmable slow cooker, but there are many programmable slow cookers I've tried that I've strongly disliked. Why? Because some go by increments of 15 or 30 minutes and some go by 4, 6, 8, or 10 hours. I dislike those restrictions, but I have family and friends who don't mind them at all! I am also pretty brand loyal when it comes to my manual slow cookers because I've had great success with those and have had unsuccessful moments with slow cookers of other brands. So, which slow cooker(s) is/are best for your household?

It really depends on how many people you're feeding and if you're gone for long periods of time. Here are my recommendations:

For 2–3 person household	3–5 quart slow cooker
For 4–5 person household	5–6 quart slow cooker
For a 6+ person household	6½–7 quart slow cooker

Large slow cooker advantages/disadvantages:

Advantages:
- You can fit a loaf pan or a baking dish into a 6- or 7-quart slow cooker, depending on the shape of your cooker. That allows you to make bread or cakes, or even smaller quantities of main dishes. (Take your favorite baking dish and loaf pan along when you shop for a cooker to make sure they'll fit inside.)
- You can feed large groups of people, or make larger quantities of food, allowing for leftovers or meals to freeze.

Disadvantages:
- They take up more storage room.
- They don't fit as neatly into a dishwasher.
- If your crock isn't ⅔–¾ full, you may burn your food.

Small slow cooker advantages/disadvantages:

Advantages:
- They're great for lots of appetizers, for serving hot drinks, for baking cakes straight in the crock, and for dorm rooms or apartments.
- Great option for making recipes of smaller quantities.

Disadvantages:
- Food in smaller quantities tends to cook more quickly than larger amounts. So keep an eye on it.
- Chances are, you won't have many leftovers. So, if you like to have leftovers, a smaller slow cooker may not be a good option for you.

My recommendation:

Have at least two slow cookers: one around 3 to 4 quarts and one 6 quarts or larger. A third would be a huge bonus (and a great advantage to your cooking repertoire!). The advantage of having at least a couple is you can make a larger variety of recipes. Also, you can make at least two or three dishes at once for a whole meal.

Manual vs. Programmable

If you are gone for only six to eight hours a day, a manual slow cooker might be just fine for you. If you are gone for more than eight hours during the day, I would highly recommend purchasing a programmable slow cooker that will switch to warm when the cook time you set is up. It will allow you to cook a wider variety of recipes.

The two I use most frequently are my 4-quart manual slow cooker and my 6½-quart programmable slow cooker. I like that I can make smaller portions in my 4-quart slow cooker on days I don't need or want leftovers, but I also love how my 6½-quart slow cooker can accommodate whole chickens, turkey breasts, hams, or big batches of soups. I use them both often.

Get to know your slow cooker . . .

Plan a little time to get acquainted with your slow cooker. Each slow cooker has its own personality—just like your oven. Plus, many new slow cookers cook hotter and faster than earlier models. I think that with all of the concern for food safety, the slow cooker manufacturers have amped up their settings so that "High," "Low," and "Warm" are all higher temperatures than in the older models. That means they cook hotter—and therefore, faster—than the first slow cookers. The beauty of these little machines is that they're supposed to cook low and slow. We count on that when we flip the switch in the morning before we leave the house for ten hours or so. So, because none of us knows what kind of temperament our slow cooker has until we try it out, nor how hot it cooks—don't assume anything. Save yourself a disappointment and make the first recipe in your new slow cooker on a day when you're at home. Cook it for the shortest amount of time the recipe calls for. Then, check the food to see if it's done. Or if you start smelling food that seems to be finished, turn off the cooker and rescue your food.

Also, all slow cookers seem to have a "hot spot," which is of great importance to know, especially when baking with your slow cooker. This spot may tend to burn food in that area if you're not careful. If you're baking directly in your slow cooker, I recommend covering the "hot spot" with some foil.

Take notes . . .

Don't be afraid to make notes in your cookbook. It's yours! Chances are, it will eventually get passed down to someone in your family and they will love and appreciate all of your musings. Take note of which slow cooker you used and exactly how long it took to cook the recipe. The next time you make it, you won't need to try to remember. Apply what you learned to the next recipes you make in your cooker. If another recipe says it needs to cook 7–9 hours, and you've discovered your slow cooker cooks on the faster side, cook that recipe for 6–6½ hours and then check it. You can always cook a recipe longer—but you can't reverse things if it's overdone.

Get creative . . .

If you know your morning is going to be hectic, prepare everything the night before, take it out so the crock warms up to room temperature when you first get up in the morning, then plug it in and turn it on as you're leaving the house.

If you want to make something that has a short cook time and you're going to be gone longer than that, cook it the night before and refrigerate it for the next day. Warm it up when you get home. Or, cook those recipes on the weekend when you know you'll be home and eat them later in the week.

Slow Cooking Tips and Tricks and Other Things You May Not Know

- Slow cookers tend to work best when they're ⅔ to ¾ of the way full. You may need to increase the cooking time if you've exceeded that amount, or reduce it if you've put in less than that. If you're going to exceed that limit, it would be best to reduce the recipe, or split it between two slow cookers. (Remember how I suggested owning at least two or three slow cookers?)
- Keep your veggies on the bottom. That puts them in more direct contact with the heat. The fuller your slow cooker, the longer it will take its contents to cook. Also, the more densely packed the cooker's contents are, the longer they will take to cook. And finally, the larger the chunks of meat or vegetables, the more time they will need to cook.
- Keep the lid on! Every time you take a peek, you lose 20 minutes of cooking time. Please take this into consideration each time you lift the lid! I know, some of you can't help yourself and are going to lift anyway. Just don't forget to tack on 20 minutes to your cook time for each time you peeked!
- Sometimes it's beneficial to remove the lid. If you'd like your dish to thicken a bit, take the lid off during the last half hour to hour of cooking time.
- If you have a big slow cooker (7- to 8-quart), you can cook a small batch in it by putting the recipe ingredients into an oven-safe baking dish or baking pan and then placing that into the cooker's crock. First, put a trivet or some metal jar rings on the bottom of the

crock, and then set your dish or pan on top of them. Or a loaf pan may "hook onto" the top ridges of the crock belonging to a large oval cooker and hang there straight and securely, "baking" a cake or quick bread. Cover the cooker and flip it on.

- The outside of your slow cooker will be hot! Please remember to keep it out of reach of children and keep that in mind for yourself as well!
- Get yourself a quick-read meat thermometer and use it! This helps remove the question of whether or not your meat is fully cooked, and helps prevent you from overcooking your meat as well.

Internal Cooking Temperatures:

- Beef—125–130°F (rare); 140–145°F (medium); 160°F (well-done)
- Pork—140–145°F (rare); 145–150°F (medium); 160°F (well-done)
- Turkey and Chicken—165°F
- Frozen meat: The basic rule of thumb is, don't put frozen meat into the slow cooker. The meat does not reach the proper internal temperature in time. This especially applies to thick cuts of meat! Proceed with caution!

- Add fresh herbs 10 minutes before the end of the cooking time to maximize their flavor.
- If your recipe calls for cooked pasta, add it 10 minutes before the end of the cooking time if the cooker is on high; 30 minutes before the end of the cooking time if it's on low. Then the pasta won't get mushy.
- If your recipe calls for sour cream or cream, stir it in 5 minutes before the end of the cooking time. You want it to heat but not boil or simmer.

Approximate Slow Cooker Temperatures (Remember, each slow cooker is different):

- High—212°F–300°F
- Low—170°F–200°F
- Simmer—185°F
- Warm—165°F

- Cooked beans freeze well. Store them in freezer bags (squeeze the air out first) or freezer boxes.

Cooked and dried bean measurements:

- 16-oz. can, drained = about 1¾ cups beans
- 19-oz. can, drained = about 2 cups beans
- 1 lb. dried beans (about 2½ cups) = 5 cups cooked beans

Breakfasts

Slow Cooker Yogurt

Becky Fixel, Grosse Pointe Farms, MI

Makes 12–14 servings

Prep. Time: 2 minutes ⚬ *Cooking Time: 12–14 hours* ⚬ *Ideal slow cooker size: 6-qt.*

I gallon whole milk

5.3 oz. Greek yogurt with cultures

1. Empty the gallon of whole milk into your slow cooker and put it on high heat for 2–4 hours. Length of time depends on your model, but the milk needs to heat to just below boiling point, about 180–200°F.

2. Turn off your slow cooker and let your milk cool down to 110–115°F. Again, this will take 2–4 hours. Set your starter Greek yogurt out so it can reach room temperature during this step.

3. In a small bowl, add about 1 cup of the warm milk and the Greek yogurt and mix together. Pour the mixture into the milk in the slow cooker and mix it in by stirring back and forth. Replace the lid of your slow cooker and wrap the whole thing in a towel. Let sit for 12–14 hours, or in other words, go to bed.

4. After 12 hours check on your glorious yogurt!

5. Line a colander with cheesecloth and place in bowl. Scoop your yogurt inside and let it sit for at least 4 hours. This will help separate the extra whey from the yogurt and thicken your final yogurt.

TIP

"My yogurt didn't all fit in one colander, but thankfully I had a second one to use. You can wait until the yogurt sinks down and there is more space in the colander if you only have one. Spoon finished yogurt into jars or containers and place in the fridge. After your yogurt is done, you're going to have leftover whey. Put it in a jar and pop it in the fridge. Use it to replace stock in recipes, water your plants, or to make cheese. It's amazing what you can do with it!"
—Becky Fixel

Calories: 190

Fat: 10g

Sodium: 130mg

Carbs: 14.5g

Sugar: 15.5g

Protein: 10g

- Gluten-Free
- Soy-Free
- Vegetarian
- Egg-Free

- High-Protein
- Low-Cal
- Low-Sodium

Chilled Peach Soup with Ginger

Annie Boshart, Lititz, PA

Makes 8 servings

Prep. Time: 45 minutes ⚓ *Cooking Time: 1 hour* ⚓ *Ideal slow cooker size: 2-qt.*

2 medium carrots, peeled and sliced

½-inch piece of peeled ginger, sliced

¾ cup plain Greek yogurt

¾ cup coconut milk

3 tsp. fresh lime juice

12–15 peaches, skins removed, cut into ½-inch pieces

3–4 oranges, squeezed for juice to make ¾ cup

dash of sea salt

dash of cayenne pepper

⅛ tsp. curry powder

2 Tbsp. fresh chopped mint

¾ cup cashews or sliced almonds, finely chopped, optional

1. Place the carrots and ginger in your crock and turn on high for 1 hour, or until ingredients are tender.

2. Place the contents of the crock in blender, puree, and allow to cool.

3. Add all remaining ingredients except nuts to blender mixture. Puree until smooth.

4. Garnish with chopped cashews or sliced almonds if desired.

Serving suggestion:

Garnish with fresh mint.

TIP

Make when local peaches are in season. Great as an appetizer for a brunch or breakfast.

Calories: 180
Fat: 6g
Sodium: 60mg
Carbs: 30.5g
Sugar: 25.5g
Protein: 5.5g

- Gluten-Free
- Vegetarian
- Low-Cal
- Low-Sodium
- Soy-Free
- Egg-Free
- Low-Fat

Pumpkin Breakfast Custard

Audrey Hess, Gettysburg, PA

Makes 4–6 servings
Prep. Time: 20 minutes ⚭ Cooking Time: 1½–2 hours ⚭ Ideal slow cooker size: 2½- or 3-qt.

2½ cups cooked, peeled, and pureed or canned pumpkin or winter squash

2 Tbsp. blackstrap molasses

3 Tbsp. maple syrup

¼ cup half-and-half

3 eggs

1 tsp. cinnamon

½ tsp. ground ginger

½ tsp. ground nutmeg

¼ tsp. ground cloves

¼ tsp. salt

1. Puree ingredients in blender until smooth.

2. Pour into greased slow cooker.

3. Cook on high for 1½–2 hours, until set in the middle and just browning at edges.

4. Serve warm in scoops over hot cereal, baked oatmeal, or as a breakfast side dish with toast or muffins.

Calories: 150
Fat: 4.5g
Sodium: 170mg
Carbs: 26g
Sugar: 14g
Protein: 4.5g

- Gluten-Free
- Vegetarian
- Soy-Free
- Low-Sodium
- Nut-Free
- Low-Fat
- Low-Cal

Grain and Fruit Cereal

Cynthia Haller, New Holland, PA

Makes 4–5 servings
Prep. Time: 5 minutes   Cooking Time: 3 hours   Ideal slow cooker size: 4-qt.

¹/₃ cup uncooked quinoa

¹/₃ cup uncooked millet

¹/₃ cup uncooked brown rice

4 cups water

¼ tsp. salt

½ cup raisins or dried cranberries

¼ cup chopped nuts, optional

1 tsp. vanilla extract, optional

½ tsp. ground cinnamon, optional

1 Tbsp. maple syrup, optional

1. Wash the quinoa, millet, and brown rice and rinse well.

2. Place the grains, water, and salt in a slow cooker. Cook on low until most of the water has been absorbed, about 3 hours.

3. Add dried fruit and any optional ingredients, and cook for 30 minutes more. If the mixture is too thick, add a little more water.

4. Serve hot or cold.

Serving suggestion:

Add a little non-dairy milk to each bowl of cereal before serving.

Calories: 220
Fat: 2g
Sodium: 150mg
Carbs: 47g
Sugar: 11g
Protein: 5.5g

- Gluten-Free
- Dairy-Free
- Soy-Free
- Vegetarian
- Vegan
- Low-Cal
- Low-Fat

Oatmeal Morning

Barbara Forrester Landis, Lititz, PA

Makes 6 servings
Prep. Time: 10 minutes & Cooking Time: 2½–6 hours & Ideal slow cooker size: 3-qt.

1 cup uncooked gluten-free
steel-cut oats

1 cup dried cranberries

1 cup walnuts

½ tsp. kosher salt

1 Tbsp. cinnamon

2 cups water

2 cups fat-free non-dairy milk
(almond, rice, etc.)

1. Combine all dry ingredients in slow cooker. Stir well.

2. Add water and milk and stir.

3. Cover. Cook on high 2½ hours, or on low 5–6 hours.

Calories: 260
Fat: 12g
Sodium: 215mg
Carbs: 38g
Sugar: 14g
Protein: 6g

- Gluten-Free
- Soy-Free
- Vegetarian
- Vegan

- Low-Sodium
- Low-Fat
- Low-Cal

Apple Oatmeal

Frances B. Musser, Newmanstown, PA

Makes 5 servings
Prep. Time: 20 minutes   ⚕   Cooking Time: 3–5 hours   ⚕   Ideal slow cooker size: 3-qt.

2 cups fat-free milk
1 cup water
1 Tbsp. honey
1 Tbsp. coconut oil
¼ tsp. kosher salt
½ tsp. cinnamon
1 cup gluten-free steel-cut oats
1 cup chopped apples
½ cup chopped walnuts
1 Tbsp. turbinado sugar

1. Grease the inside of the slow cooker crock.

2. Add all ingredients to crock and mix.

3. Cover. Cook on low 3–5 hours.

Calories: 220
Fat: 12g
Sodium: 160mg
Carbs: 28.5g
Sugar: 14g
Protein: 8.5g

- Gluten-Free
- Vegetarian
- Low-Cal

- Low-Sodium
- Soy-Free
- Egg-Free

Overnight Oat Groats

Rebekah Zehr, Lowville, NY

Makes 6 servings
Prep. Time: 5 minutes ⚜ Cooking Time: 8–10 hours ⚜ Ideal slow cooker size: 3-qt.

1½ cups gluten-free oat groats

4 cups water

2 cups almond milk

1–2 cinnamon sticks

⅓ cup maple syrup

½–1 cup dried apples

2 scoops gluten-free vanilla-flavored protein powder, optional

1. Combine all ingredients in slow cooker.

2. Cook on low for 8–10 hours.

3. Remove cinnamon sticks and serve while warm.

Calories: 160
Fat: 2.5g
Sodium: 65mg
Carbs: 39.5g
Sugar: 22g
Protein: 4.5g

- Gluten-Free
- Dairy-Free
- Vegan
- Vegetarian

- Soy-Free
- Low-Sodium
- Low-Cal

Five Grain Slow Cooker Breakfast

Dena Mell-Dorchy, Royal Oak, MI

Makes 8 servings

Prep. Time: 15 minutes   ⚜   Cooking Time: 6–7 hours   ⚜   Ideal slow cooker size: 3- or 4-qt.

5 cups of water

1 cup of dried fruit and nuts
(cranberries, cherries, raisins, pineapple,
coconut, pecans, and/or walnuts)

¼ cup crystalized ginger

3 Tbsp. gluten-free oats

3 Tbsp. quinoa

3 Tbsp. brown rice

2 Tbsp. flaxseeds

2 Tbsp. gluten-free cornmeal

1 tsp. vanilla

1 tsp. cinnamon

1 Tbsp. hemp seeds, optional

Optional toppings: milk, yogurt,
turbinado sugar, maple syrup, honey

1. Spray slow cooker with non-stick spray.

2. Combine all ingredients (except optional toppings) in slow cooker, cover, and cook on low setting for 6–7 hours.

3. Serve with any of the optional toppings, if desired. If keeping recipe vegan, avoid topping with dairy milk, yogurt, or honey.

Calories: 180
Fat: 8g
Sodium: 10mg
Carbs: 24g
Sugar: 9.5g
Protein: 5g

- Gluten-Free
- Vegan
- Vegetarian
- Soy-Free

- Low-Cal
- Low-Fat
- Low-Sodium
- Low-Sugar

Warm 'n Fruity

Marlene Weaver, Lititz, PA

Makes 10 cups
Prep. Time: 10 minutes ⚜ Cooking Time: 6–7 hours ⚜ Ideal slow cooker size: 5-qt.

5 cups water
2 cups seven-grain cereal
1 medium apple, peeled and chopped
1 cup unsweetened apple juice
¼ cup dried apricots, chopped
¼ cup dried cranberries
¼ cup raisins
¼ cup chopped dates
¼ cup maple syrup
1 teaspoon cinnamon
½ teaspoon salt
Chopped walnuts, optional

1. In the crock, combine all ingredients except for walnuts.

2. Cover and cook on low for 6–7 hours or until fruits are softened.

3. Sprinkle individual servings with walnuts if desired.

Calories: 100
Fat: 0g
Sodium: 150mg
Carbs: 26.5g
Sugar: 16g
Protein: 1.5g

- Dairy-Free
- Low-Fat
- Soy-Free
- Egg-Free
- Vegetarian
- Vegan
- Low-Cal

Apple Breakfast Cobbler

Anona M. Teel, Bangor, PA

Makes 8 servings
Prep. Time: 25 minutes ⚬ *Cooking Time: 2–9 hours* ⚬ *Ideal slow cooker size: 4- or 5-qt.*

8 medium apples, cored, peeled, sliced
2 Tbsp. maple syrup
dash of cinnamon
juice of 1 lemon
2 Tbsp. coconut oil, melted
2 cups homemade granola

1. Combine ingredients in slow cooker.

2. Cover. Cook on low 7–9 hours (while you sleep!), or on high 2–3 hours (after you're up in the morning).

Calories: 210
Fat: 18.5g
Sodium: 20mg
Carbs: 61g
Sugar: 34g
Protein: 9.5g

- Gluten-Free
- Dairy-Free
- Soy-Free
- Vegetarian

- Vegan
- Low-Sodium
- Low-Cal

Apple Granola

Phyllis Good, Lancaster, PA

Makes 12 servings

Prep. Time: 20 minutes ⚶ Cooking Time: 1½–2 hours ⚶ Chilling time: 1 hour ⚶ Ideal slow cooker size: 5-qt.

9 cups unpeeled, sliced apples

1½ tsp. cinnamon

1½ cups dry rolled oats

1½ cups wheat germ

1½ cups whole wheat flour

1½ cups sunflower seeds

1⅓ cups water

¾ cup honey

1. Grease interior of slow cooker crock.

2. Use your food processor to slice the apples. Place slices in slow cooker.

3. Sprinkle apple slices with cinnamon, and then stir together gently.

4. In a good-sized bowl, stir together dry oats, wheat germ, whole wheat flour, and sunflower seeds.

5. When dry ingredients are well mixed, pour in water and honey. Using a sturdy spoon or your clean hands, mix thoroughly until wet ingredients are damp throughout.

6. Spoon over apples.

7. Cover, but vent the lid by propping it open with a chopstick or wooden spoon handle. Or if you're using an oval cooker, turn the lid sideways.

8. Cook on high for 1 hour, stirring up from the bottom and around the sides every 20 minutes or so. (Set a timer so you don't forget!)

9. Switch the cooker to Low. Bake another 1–2 hours, still stirring every 20 minutes or so.

10. Granola is done when it eventually browns a bit and looks dry.

11. Pour granola onto parchment or a large baking sheet to cool and crisp up more.

12. If you like clumps, no need to stir granola further while it cools. Otherwise, break up the granola with a spoon or your hands as it cools.

13. When completely cooled, store in airtight container.

Calories: 350

Fat: 11.5g

Sodium: 10mg

Carbs: 57.5g

Sugar: 26.5g

Protein: 10.5g

• Vegetarian
• Low-Sodium

Soy-Flax Granola

Phyllis Good, Lancaster, PA

Makes 15 servings

Prep. Time: 20 minutes   ⚜   Cooking Time: 1½–2½ hours   ⚜   Chilling Time: 2 hours   ⚜   Ideal slow cooker size: 6-qt.

12 oz. soybeans, roasted with no salt

4 cups gluten-free rolled oats

¾ cup soy flour

¾ cup ground flaxseeds

1 tsp. salt

2 tsp. cinnamon

⅔ cup coarsely chopped walnuts

⅔ cup whole pecans

¾ cup maple syrup

½ cup coconut oil, melted

¾ cup applesauce

2 tsp. vanilla

Optional additions: dried cranberries, dried cherries, chopped dried apricots, chopped dried figs, raisins, or some combination of these dried fruits

Calories: 430
Fat: 25.5g
Sodium: 160mg
Carbs: 40g
Sugar: 12g
Protein: 15g

- Gluten-Free
- Dairy-Free
- Low-Salt
- Low-Sodium

1. Grease interior of slow cooker crock.

2. Briefly process soybeans in a blender or food processor until coarsely chopped. Place in large bowl.

3. Add oats, flour, flaxseeds, salt, cinnamon, walnuts, and pecans. Mix thoroughly with spoon.

4. In a smaller bowl, combine maple syrup, coconut oil, applesauce, and vanilla well.

5. Pour wet ingredients over dry. Stir well, remembering to stir up from the bottom, using either a strong spoon or your clean hands.

6. Pour mixture into crock. Cover, but vent the lid by propping it open with a chopstick or wooden spoon handle. Or if you're using an oval cooker, turn the lid sideways.

7. Cook on high for 1 hour, stirring up from the bottom and around the sides every 20 minutes or so. (Set a timer so you don't forget!)

8. Switch the cooker to Low. Bake another 1–2 hours, still stirring every 20 minutes.

9. Granola is done when it eventually browns a bit and looks dry.

10. Pour granola onto parchment or a large baking sheet to cool and crisp up more.

11. Stir in any of the dried fruits that you want.

12. If you like clumps, no need to stir granola again while it cools. Otherwise, break up the granola with a spoon or your hands as it cools.

13. When completely cooled, store in airtight container.

Granola in the Slow Cooker

Earnie Zimmerman, Mechanicsburg, PA

Makes 10–12 servings
Prep. Time: 10 minutes   ♣   Cooking Time: 3–8 hours   ♣   Ideal slow cooker size: 6-qt.

5 cups gluten-free rolled oats
1 Tbsp. flaxseeds
¼ cup slivered almonds
¼ cup chopped pecans or walnuts
¼ cup unsweetened shredded coconut
¼ cup maple syrup or honey
½ cup dried fruit
¼ cup melted coconut oil

1. Spray slow cooker crock with cooking spray. In slow cooker, mix together oats, flaxseeds, almonds, pecans or walnuts, and coconut.

2. Separately, combine maple syrup or honey and coconut oil. Pour over dry ingredients in cooker and toss well.

3. Place lid on slow cooker with a wooden spoon handle or chopstick venting one end of the lid.

4. Cook on high for 3–4 hours, stirring every 30 minutes, or cook on low for 8 hours, stirring every hour. You may need to stir more often or cook for less time, depending on how hot your cooker cooks.

5. When Granola smells good and toasty, pour it out onto a baking sheet to cool.

6. Add dried fruit to cooled Granola and store in airtight container.

Calories: 260
Fat: 11.5g
Sodium: 5mg
Carbs: 35g
Sugar: 8g
Protein: 6g

- Gluten-Free
- Dairy-Free
- Low-Sodium
- Soy-Free
- Low-Sugar

Sweet Potatoes Ole

Hope Comerford, Clinton Township, MI

Makes 8 servings
Prep. Time: 10 minutes ⚬ Cooking Time: 6 hours ⚬ Ideal slow cooker size: 5- or 6-qt.

4 lbs. sweet potatoes, peeled and diced

15-oz. can black beans, drained, rinsed

1 cup chopped onion

4-oz. can diced green chilies

8 eggs

½ cup salsa

½ cup shredded Monterey Jack cheese

1. Spray crock with non-stick spray.

2. In crock, mix together sweet potatoes, black beans, onion, and diced green chilies.

3. In a bowl, mix together the eggs, salsa, and Monterey Jack cheese. Pour over the sweet potatoes.

4. Cover and cook on low for 6 hours.

Calories: 350
Fat: 7g
Sodium: 500mg
Carbs: 58.5g
Sugar: 11.5g
Protein: 14.5g

- Gluten-Free
- Vegetarian
- Soy-Free
- High-Protein
- Nut-Free
- Low-Fat

Fiesta Hashbrowns

Dena Mell-Dorchy, Royal Oak, MI

Makes 8 servings

Prep. Time: 15 minutes ☙ *Cooking Time: 8–9 hours* ☙ *Ideal slow cooker size: 3- or 4-qt.*

1 lb. ground turkey sausage

½ cup chopped onion

5 cups gluten-free frozen diced hash browns

8 oz. gluten-free low sodium chicken stock

1 small red sweet pepper

1 jalapeño, seeded and finely diced

1½ cups sliced mushrooms

2 Tbsp. quick cooking tapioca

½ cup shredded Monterey Jack cheese

1. Spray slow cooker with non-stick spray.

2. In a large skillet, brown sausage and onion over medium heat. Drain off fat.

3. Combine sausage mixture, hash browns, chicken stock, sweet pepper, jalapeño, mushrooms, and quick cooking tapioca in cooker; stir to combine.

4. Cover and cook on low heat for 8–9 hours. Stir before serving. Top with shredded Monterey Jack cheese.

Calories: 275
Fat: 10g
Sodium: 500mg
Carbs: 29g
Sugar: 2g
Protein: 18g

- Gluten-Free
- Soy-Free
- Nut-Free
- Low-Fat
- Low-Cal

Huevos Rancheros in Crock

Pat Bishop, Bedminster, PA

Makes 6 servings

Prep. Time: 25 minutes 🍳 Cooking Time: 2 hours 🍳 Ideal slow cooker size: 6-qt.

3 cups gluten-free salsa, room temperature

2 cups cooked beans, drained, room temperature

6 eggs, room temperature

salt and pepper to taste

1/3 cup grated Mexican-blend cheese, optional

6 white corn tortillas, for serving

1. Mix salsa and beans in slow cooker.

2. Cook on high for 1 hour or until steaming.

3. With a spoon, make 6 evenly spaced dents in the salsa mixture; try not to expose the bottom of the crock. Break an egg into each dent.

4. Salt and pepper eggs. Sprinkle with cheese if you wish.

5. Cover and continue to cook on high until egg whites are set and yolks are as firm as you like them, approximately 20–40 minutes.

6. To serve, scoop out an egg with some beans and salsa. Serve with warm tortillas.

Calories: 200
Fat: 1g
Sodium: 975mg
Carbs: 36g
Sugar: 6g
Protein: 12g

- Gluten-Free
- Soy-Free
- Low-Cal

- Low-Fat
- Nut-Free
- Vegetarian

Spanish Breakfast "Skillet"

Hope Comerford, Clinton Township, MI

Makes 6 servings
Prep. Time: 25 minutes   Cooking Time: 5–6 hours   Ideal slow cooker size: 5- or 6-qt.

I lb. turkey sausage, browned, drained

I 4.5-oz. pkg. tostada shells, broken coarsely

I medium red bell pepper, chopped

I medium onion, chopped

I 4-oz. can diced green chilies

I cup almond milk

12 eggs

I tsp. sea salt

¼ tsp. black pepper

½ cup crumbled queso fresco

Optional toppings: 2 sliced avocados, 8 oz. non-fat Greek yogurt, 2 cups salsa

1. Spray crock with non-stick spray.

2. In crock, combine browned sausage, tostada pieces, red bell pepper, onion, and green chilies.

3. In a large bowl mix together the almond milk, eggs, sea salt, and black pepper.

4. Pour egg mixture over sausage mixture in crock.

5. Sprinkle crumbled queso fresco over the top.

6. Cover and cook on low for 5–6 hours.

Serving suggestion:

Garnish with pico de gallo.

Calories: 290
Fat: 17g
Sodium: 1070mg
Carbs: 17g
Sugar: 2g
Protein: 20g

- Gluten-Free
- Low-Carb
- Low-Cal
- Low-Sodium

- Soy-Free
- High-Protein
- Low-Sugar

Italian Frittata

Hope Comerford, Clinton Township, MI

Makes 6 servings
Prep. Time: 10 minutes   ⚬   Cooking Time: 3–4 hours   ⚬   Ideal slow cooker size: 5- or 6-qt.

10 eggs
1 Tbsp. chopped fresh basil
1 Tbsp. chopped fresh mint
1 Tbsp. chopped fresh sage
1 Tbsp. chopped fresh oregano
½ tsp. sea salt
⅛ tsp. pepper
1 Tbsp. grated Parmesan cheese
¼ cup diced prosciutto
½ cup chopped onion

1. Spray your crock with non-stick spray.

2. In a bowl, mix together the eggs, basil, mint, sage, oregano, sea salt, pepper, and Parmesan. Pour this mixture into the crock.

3. Sprinkle the prosciutto and onion evenly over the egg mixture in the crock.

4. Cover and cook on low for 3–4 hours.

Calories: 145
Fat: 9g
Sodium: 370mg
Carbs: 2.5g
Sugar: 1g
Protein: 12.5g

- Gluten-Free
- Low-Carb
- Low-Cal
- Low-Sugar

- Soy-Free
- Nut-Free
- Low-Sodium
- Paleo

Spinach Fritatta

Shirley Unternahrer, Wayland, IA

Makes 4–6 servings
Prep. Time: 15 minutes   ♣   Cooking Time: 1½–2 hours   ♣   Ideal slow cooker size: 5-qt.

4 eggs

½ tsp. kosher salt

½ tsp. dried basil

fresh ground pepper, to taste

3 cups chopped fresh spinach, stems removed

½ cup chopped tomato, liquid drained off

⅓ cup freshly grated Parmesan cheese

1. Whisk eggs well in mixing bowl. Whisk in salt, basil, and pepper.

2. Gently stir in spinach, tomato, and Parmesan.

3. Pour into lightly greased slow cooker.

4. Cover and cook on high for 1½–2 hours, until middle is set. Serve hot.

Calories: 90
Fat: 5.5g
Sodium: 420mg
Carbs: 3g
Sugar: .5g
Protein: 7g

- Gluten-Free
- Soy-Free
- Vegetarian
- Low-Sugar

- Low-Fat
- Low-Cal
- Nut-Free

Crustless Spinach Quiche

Barbara Hoover, Landisville, PA

Makes 8 servings
Prep. Time: 15 minutes 🍃 Cooking Time: 2–4 hours 🍃 Ideal slow cooker size: 3- or 4-qt.

2 10-oz. pkgs. frozen chopped spinach
2 cups cottage cheese
¼ cup coconut oil
1½ cups sharp cheddar cheese, cubed
3 eggs, beaten
¼ cup all-purpose gluten-free flour
1 tsp. salt

1. Grease interior of slow cooker crock.

2. Thaw spinach completely. Squeeze as dry as you can. Then place in crock.

3. Stir in all other ingredients and combine well.

4. Cover. Cook on low 2–4 hours, or until quiche is set. Stick blade of knife into center of quiche. If blade comes out clean, quiche is set. If it doesn't, cover and cook another 15 minutes or so.

5. When cooked, allow to stand 10–15 minutes so mixture can firm up. Then serve.

Calories: 250
Fat: 18.5g
Sodium: 675mg
Carbs: 7.5g
Sugar: 2.5g
Protein: 15.5g

- Gluten-Free
- High-Protein
- Soy-Free
- Low-Cal
- Low-Sugar

Appetizers & Snacks

Slow-Cooked Salsa

Andy Wagner, Quarryville, PA

Makes 2 cups

Prep. Time: 15 minutes ❧ Cooking Time: 1½–3 hours ❧ Standing Time: 2 hours ❧
Ideal slow cooker size: 3-qt.

10 plum tomatoes

2 garlic cloves

1 small onion, cut into wedges

1–2 jalapeño peppers

½ cup chopped fresh cilantro

½ tsp. sea salt, optional

1. Core tomatoes. Cut a small slit in two tomatoes. Insert a garlic clove into each slit.

2. Place all tomatoes and onions in a 3-qt. slow cooker.

3. Cut stems off jalapeños. (Remove seeds if you want a milder salsa.) Place jalapeños in the slow cooker.

4. Cover and cook on high for 2½–3 hours or until vegetables are softened. Some may brown slightly. Cool at least 2 hours with the lid off.

5. In a blender, combine the tomato mixture, cilantro, and salt if you wish. Cover and process until blended.

6. Refrigerate leftovers.

Serving suggestion:

Garnish with cilantro and jalapeño.

TIP

Wear disposable gloves when cutting hot peppers; the oils can burn your skin. Avoid touching your face when you've been working with hot peppers.

Per ¼ cup:
Calories: 60
Fat: 0g
Sodium: 10mg
Carbs: 15g
Sugar: 13.5g
Protein: .5g

- Gluten-Free
- Dairy-Free
- Vegetarian
- Vegan
- Low-Sodium

- Low-Fat
- Nut-Free
- Soy-Free
- Low-Cal

Mexican Dip

Marla Folkerts, Holland, OH

Makes 15 servings
Prep. Time: 15–20 minutes ⚹ Cooking Time: 2-3 hours ⚹ Ideal slow cooker size: 3-qt.

1 lb. low-fat ground beef or turkey

8-oz. pkg. low-fat Mexican cheese, grated

16-oz. jar mild, thick, and chunky picante salsa, or thick and chunky salsa

6-oz. can vegetarian refried beans

1. Brown meat in nonstick skillet.

2. Place meat and remaining ingredients into your crock and stir.

3. Cover and cook on low for 3 hours, or until all ingredients are heated through and melted.

Serving suggestion:
Garnish with jalapeño.

Calories: 89
Fat: 4g
Sodium: 400mg
Carbs: 5g
Sugar: 2g
Protein: 9g

- Gluten-Free
- Soy-Free
- Vegetarian
- Low-Fat
- Nut-Free
- Low-Cal
- Low-Sugar

Seafood Dip

Joan Rosenberger, Stephens City, VA

Makes 24 servings of 2 Tbsp. each
Prep. Time: 5–10 minutes   ⚶   Cooking Time: 3 hours   ⚶   Ideal slow cooker size: 3½-qt.

10-oz. pkg. fat-free cream cheese
8-oz. pkg. imitation crab strands
2 Tbsp. onion, finely chopped
4–5 drops hot sauce
¼ cup walnuts, finely chopped
1 tsp. paprika

1. Blend all ingredients except nuts and paprika until well mixed.

2. Spread in slow cooker. Sprinkle with nuts and paprika.

3. Cook on low 3 hours.

Serving suggestion:
Garnish with paprika or cayenne pepper and parsley or cilantro.

Calories: 30
Fat: 1g
Sodium: 130mg
Carbs: 2.5g
Sugar: 1.5g
Protein: 3g

- Gluten-Free
- Vegetarian
- Soy-Free

- Low-Fat
- Low-Cal
- Low-Sugar

Zesty Pizza Dip

Hope Comerford, Clinton Township, MI

Makes 14 servings
Prep. Time: 15 minutes & Cooking Time: 5–6 hours & Ideal slow cooker size: 3½- or 4-qt.

1 lb. bulk gluten-free turkey sausage
⅔ cup chopped onion
4 cloves garlic, minced
2 15-oz. cans low-sodium tomato sauce
14.5-oz. can diced tomatoes
6-oz. can low-sodium tomato paste
1 Tbsp. dried oregano
1 Tbsp. dried basil
¾ tsp. crushed red pepper
1½ tsp. turbinado sugar
½ cup sliced black olives

1. In a large skillet, brown the turkey sausage, onion, and garlic. Drain the grease.

2. In the crock, combine all the remaining ingredients except the olives.

3. Cover and cook on low for 5–6 hours. Just before serving, stir in the olives.

Serving suggestion:
To keep this nice and healthy, serve with a rainbow of bell pepper slices to dip with. Garnish with microgreens or chopped parsley.

Calories: 95
Fat: 3g
Sodium: 260mg
Carbs: 10g
Sugar: 6g
Protein: 8g

- Gluten-Free
- Dairy-Free
- Soy-Free
- Nut-Free

- Low-Cal
- Low-Fat
- Low-Sugar

Lightened-Up Spinach Artichoke Dip

Hope Comerford, Clinton Township, MI

Makes 6–8 servings

Prep. Time: 10 minutes ⚜ Cooking Time: 3–4 hours ⚜ Ideal slow cooker size: 3- or 4-qt.

10-oz. bag fresh baby spinach, roughly chopped

13.75-oz. can quartered artichoke hearts, drained and chopped

8-oz. brick reduced-fat cream cheese

1 cup non-fat plain Greek yogurt

1 cup shredded mozzarella cheese

½ cup grated Parmesan cheese

½ cup chopped onion

¼ cup chopped green onion

1. Spray your crock with non-stick spray.

2. Combine all ingredients in crock, making sure everything is well-mixed.

3. Cover and cook on low for 3–4 hours, or until the cheese is melted and the dip is heated all the way through.

Serving suggestion:

Serve with brown rice crackers, gluten-free pita bread, or fresh carrot sticks. Garnish with thinly sliced red bell pepper.

Calories: 200
Fat: 12g
Sodium: 490mg
Carbs: 7g
Sugar: 5g
Protein: 13g

- Gluten-Free
- Vegetarian
- Low-Sugar

- High-Protein
- Nut-Free
- Low-Cal

Seven Layer Dip

Hope Comerford, Clinton Township, MI

Makes 10–15 servings
Prep. Time: 20 minutes ⚜ Cooking Time: 2 hours ⚜ Ideal slow cooker size: 6-qt.

1 lb. lean ground turkey

2½ tsp. chili powder, divided

½ tsp. kosher salt

⅛ tsp. pepper

15-oz. can fat-free refried beans

4-oz. can diced green chilies

1 cup non-fat Greek yogurt

1 cup salsa

1 cup shredded Mexican blend cheese

2-oz. can sliced black olives

2 green onions, sliced

1. Brown the ground turkey with 1 tsp. chili powder, salt, and pepper.

2. Meanwhile spray the crock with non-stick spray.

3. Mix together 1 tsp. chili powder with the refried beans, then spread them into a layer at the bottom of the crock.

4. Next add a layer of the diced green chilies.

5. Spread the ground turkey over the top of the green chilies.

6. Mix together the remaining ½ tsp. chili powder with the Greek yogurt, and then spread this over the ground turkey in the crock.

7. Next, spread the salsa over the top.

8. Last, sprinkle the cheese into a layer on top and end with the black olives.

9. Cover and cook on low for 2 hours. Sprinkle the green onions on top before serving.

Calories: 135
Fat: 6g
Sodium: 420mg
Carbs: 11g
Sugar: 2g
Protein: 12g

- Gluten-Free
- Low-Carb
- Low-Fat
- Low-Sodium
- Soy-Free
- Low-Sugar
- Low-Cal

Prairie Fire Dip

Cheri Jantzen, Houston, TX

Makes 1¼ cups, or 10 servings
Prep. Time: 5–10 minutes ♣ Cooking Time: 1–3 hours ♣ Ideal slow cooker size: 2-qt.

1 cup vegetarian refried fat-free beans
(half a 15-oz. can)

½ cup shredded fat-free Monterey Jack
cheese

¼ cup water

1 Tbsp. minced onion

1 clove garlic, minced

2 tsp. chili powder

hot sauce as desired

1. Combine all ingredients in slow cooker.

2. Cover. Cook on high 1 hour, or on low 2–3 hours. Serve with baked tortilla chips.

Serving suggestion:
Garnish with hot sauce and diced avocado.

Calories: 34
Fat: 1g
Sodium: 140mg
Carbs: 5g
Sugar: 0g
Protein: 3g

- Gluten-Free
- Vegetarian
- Soy-Free
- Nut-Free

- Low-Fat
- Low-Cal
- Low-Carb
- Sugar-Free

Chicken Lettuce Wraps

Hope Comerford, Clinton Township, MI

Makes About 12 wraps

Prep. Time: 15 minutes ⚶ Cooking Time: 2–3 hours ⚶ Ideal slow cooker size: 5- or 7-qt.

2 lbs. ground chicken, browned

4 cloves garlic, minced

½ cup minced sweet yellow onion

4 Tbsp. gluten-free soy sauce or Bragg's liquid aminos

1 Tbsp. natural crunchy peanut butter

1 tsp. rice wine vinegar

1 tsp. sesame oil

¼ tsp. kosher salt

¼ tsp. red pepper flakes

¼ tsp. black pepper

8-oz. can sliced water chestnuts, drained, rinsed, chopped

3 green onions, sliced

12 good-sized pieces of iceberg lettuce, rinsed and patted dry

1. In the crock, combine the ground chicken, garlic, yellow onion, soy sauce or liquid aminos, peanut butter, vinegar, sesame oil, salt, red pepper flakes, and black pepper.

2. Cover and cook on low for 2–3 hours.

3. Add in the water chestnuts and green onions. Cover and cook for an additional 10–15 minutes.

4. Serve a good spoonful on each piece of iceberg lettuce.

Serving suggestion:

Garnish with diced red bell pepper and diced green onion.

Calories: 135
Fat: 7g
Sodium: 430mg
Carbs: 3.5g
Sugar: 1g
Protein: 14.5g

- Gluten-Free
- Dairy-Free
- Low-Carb
- Low-Cal

- Egg-Free
- Low-Fat
- Low-Sugar

Tempting Tiny Turkey Meatballs

Hope Comerford, Clinton Township, MI

Makes 40–50 tiny meatballs

Prep. Time: 30 minutes ⚬ Cooking Time: 6 hours ⚬ Ideal slow cooker size: 6- or 7-qt.

2 lbs. lean ground turkey

⅔ cup cooked quinoa

6 cloves garlic, minced, divided

1 egg lightly beaten

2 Tbsp. grated Parmesan

3 Tbsp. Italian seasoning, divided

3 tsp. onion powder, divided

1¾ tsp. kosher salt

1 tsp. pepper, divided

4 Tbsp. olive oil

2 28-oz. cans low-sodium crushed tomatoes

6-oz. can low-sodium tomato paste

¼ cup balsamic vinegar

1. Mix together the ground turkey, quinoa, 3 cloves minced garlic, egg, Parmesan cheese, 1 Tbsp. Italian seasoning, 1 tsp. onion powder, ¾ tsp. kosher salt, and ½ tsp. pepper. Form this into tiny ½" meatballs.

2. In a large skillet over medium-high heat, heat 2 Tbsp. of olive oil and gently sear all sides of each meatball. Set them aside.

3. In a large bowl, mix together the crushed tomatoes, tomato paste, remaining 3 cloves of minced garlic, 2 Tbsp. Italian seasoning, 2 tsp. onion powder, 1 tsp. kosher salt, ½ tsp. pepper, 2 Tbsp. olive oil, and ¼ cup balsamic vinegar.

4. Pour half the tomato sauce mixture into the crock; gently add all of the tiny meatballs. Finish by pouring the rest of the tomato sauce over the top.

5. Cover and cook on low for 6 hours.

Serving suggestion:

Garnish with diced green onion or diced fresh basil and serve with fun decorative toothpicks.

Per 3 tiny meatballs:
Calories: 175
Fat: 10g
Sodium: 350mg
Carbs: 10g
Sugar: 5g
Protein: 14g

- Gluten-Free
- Soy-Free
- Low-Sodium
- Low-Cal
- Low-Sugar

Mouthwatering Sausage Bites

Hope Comerford, Clinton Township, MI

Makes 18–20 servings
Prep. Time: 15 minutes ❧ Cooking Time: 4–6 hours ❧ Ideal slow cooker size: 2½- or 3-qt.

1 medium sweet yellow onion, sliced

2 sweet apples, peeled, cored, sliced

2 lbs. chicken apple sausage links, sliced into ½" rounds

4 Tbsp. spicy brown mustard

4 Tbsp. balsamic vinegar

⅓ cup honey

1. Spray your crock with non-stick spray.

2. Place the onions and apples in the bottom of the crock, topped with the sausages.

3. In a bowl, mix together the mustard, balsamic vinegar, and honey. Pour this over the contents of the slow cooker.

4. Cover and cook on low for 4–6 hours. Serve with toothpicks.

Calories: 125
Fat: 4g
Sodium: 320mg
Carbs: 13g
Sugar: 13g
Protein: 8g

- Gluten-Free
- Dairy-Free
- Soy-Free
- Nut-Free
- Low-Fat
- Low-Cal

Tomato-Zucchini Ratatouille

Barb Yoder, Angola, IN

Makes about 3½ cups, or 13 servings

Prep. Time: 20–30 minutes   ♣   Cooking Time: 7–8 hours   ♣   Ideal slow cooker size: 4-qt.

1½ cups chopped onion

6-oz. can tomato paste

1 Tbsp. olive oil

2 cloves garlic, minced (1 tsp.)

1½ tsp. crushed dried basil

½ tsp. dried thyme

15-oz. can chopped low-sodium tomatoes, with juice drained but reserved

1 large zucchini, halved lengthwise and sliced thin

salt and pepper to taste, optional

26 slices French bread or baguette

1. Mix all ingredients except bread in slow cooker.

2. Cover. Cook on low 7–8 hours.

3. If mixture is stiffer than you wish, stir in some reserved tomato juice.

4. Serve hot or cold on top of French bread or baguette slices.

Calories: 200
Fat: 3.5g
Sodium: 260mg
Carbs: 37g
Sugar: 5g
Protein: 7g

- Vegetarian
- Vegan
- Low-Sodium
- Soy-Free

- Nut-Free
- Low-Cal
- Low-Fat
- Low-Sugar

Garlicky Hoisin Mushrooms

Hope Comerford, Clinton Township, MI

Makes 10 servings
Prep. Time: 10 minutes ❧ Cooking Time: 5–6 hours ❧ Ideal slow cooker size: 3-qt.

24 oz. whole button mushrooms, trimmed

1 small sweet onion, halved, sliced

¼ cup of water

3 cloves garlic, minced

2 Tbsp. gluten-free soy sauce or Bragg's liquid aminos

1 Tbsp. smooth natural peanut butter

1 tsp. rice wine vinegar

1 tsp. sesame oil

¼ tsp. crushed red pepper

1. Spray crock with non-stick spray.

2. Place mushrooms and onions into the crock.

3. In a bowl, mix together the water, garlic, soy sauce, peanut butter, rice wine vinegar, sesame oil, and crushed red pepper. Pour this mixture over the mushrooms and onions.

4. Cover and cook on low for 5–6 hours.

5. To serve, stir the mushrooms gently through the sauce, then remove with a slotted spoon. Serve the mushrooms with toothpicks.

Serving suggestion:
Garnish with diced green onion and sesame seeds.

Calories: 45
Fat: 1.5g
Sodium: 200mg
Carbs: 5.5g
Sugar: 3g
Protein: 3g

- Gluten-Free
- Vegetarian
- Vegan
- Low-Cal
- Low-Fat
- Low-Carb
- Low-Sugar
- Low-Sodium

Artichokes

Susan Yoder Graber, Eureka, IL

Makes 4 servings
Prep. Time: 20 minutes & Cooking Time: 2–10 hours & Ideal slow cooker size: 3-qt.

4 artichokes
1 tsp. salt
2 Tbsp. lemon juice

1. Wash and trim artichokes by cutting off the stems flush with the bottoms of the artichokes and by cutting ¾–1 inch off the tops. Stand upright in slow cooker.

2. Mix together salt and lemon juice and pour over artichokes.

3. Pour in water to cover ¾ of artichokes.

4. Cover. Cook on low 8–10 hours, or high 2–4 hours.

Serving suggestion:

Serve with melted butter. Pull off individual leaves and dip bottom of each into butter. Using your teeth, strip the individual leaf off the meaty portion at the bottom of each leaf.

Calories: 80
Fat: .5g
Sodium: 700mg
Carbs: 17.5g
Sugar: 2g
Protein: 5.5g

- Gluten-Free
- Dairy-Free
- Soy-Free
- Nut-Free
- Low-Fat

- Low-Cal
- Low-Sugar
- Vegan
- Vegetarian

Southern Boiled Peanuts

Mary June Hershberger, Lynchburg, VA

Makes 32 servings

Prep. Time: 5 minutes & Cooking Time: 7–8 hours & Standing Time: 8 hours or overnight &
Ideal slow cooker size: 5-qt.

2 lbs. raw peanuts in the shell

7 Tbsp. salt

water to cover peanuts

1. Wash unshelled peanuts in water until the water is clear.

2. In your slow cooker crock, soak peanuts overnight in water to cover with 7 Tbsp. salt.

3. In the morning, turn cooker to low and cook for 7–10 hours until peanuts are desired tenderness. Boiled peanuts should be tender, not crunchy hard, and the shells will be quite soft.

4. Drain peanuts and allow to cool 10 minutes before serving. Peel shells off peanuts and eat.

5. Store leftover boiled peanuts in refrigerator, or freeze. Reheat before eating.

Calories: 170
Fat: 13g
Sodium: 540mg
Carbs: 7g
Sugar: 0g
Protein: 7g

- Gluten-Free
- Vegan
- Vegetarian
- Soy-Free
- Sugar-Free
- High-Protein
- Low-Carb
- Low-Cal

Sweet-and-Hot Mixed Nuts

Hope Comerford, Clinton Township, MI

Makes 22 servings (about ¼ cup each)

Prep. Time: 15 minutes ☙ Cooking Time: 2 hours ☙ Cooling Time: 1 hour ☙ Ideal slow cooker size: 2- or 3-qt.

I cup unsalted cashews

I cup unsalted almonds

I cup unsalted pecans

I cup unsalted, shelled pistachios

½ cup maple syrup

⅓ cup melted coconut oil

I tsp. ground ginger

½ tsp. sea salt

½ tsp. cinnamon

¼ tsp. ground cloves

¼ tsp. cayenne pepper

1. Spray crock with non-stick spray.

2. Place nuts in the crock and combine them with all the remaining ingredients, making sure all nuts are coated evenly.

3. Before covering the crock, place a piece of paper towel or thin dishtowel under the lid. Cook on low for 1 hour and then stir the nuts. At 2 hours, stir again and then lay them on a parchment paper-lined cookie sheet. Let them cool for 1 hour.

4. Serve or store any remaining nuts in a covered container for up to 3 weeks.

Calories: 180
Fat: 15g
Sodium: 55mg
Carbs: 10.5g
Sugar: 5.5g
Protein: 4g

- Gluten-Free
- Dairy-Free
- Vegetarian
- Vegan
- Low-Sodium

- High-Protein
- Soy-Free
- Low-Cal
- Low-Sugar

Curried Almonds

Barbara Aston, Ashdown, AR

Makes 64 servings (1 Tbsp. each)

Prep. Time: 5 minutes & *Cooking Time: 3½–4½ hours* & *Ideal slow cooker size: 3-qt.*

2 Tbsp. coconut oil

1 Tbsp. curry powder

½ tsp. sea salt

⅛ tsp. turmeric

⅛ tsp. paprika

⅛ tsp. onion powder

⅛ tsp. garlic powder

⅛ tsp. sugar

1 lb. blanched almonds

1. Combine coconut oil with spices.

2. Pour over almonds in slow cooker. Mix to coat well.

3. Cover. Cook on low 2–3 hours. Turn to high. Uncover cooker and cook 1–1½ hours.

4. Serve warm or at room temperature.

Calories: 50

Fat: 4g

Sodium: 20mg

Carbs: 1.5g

Sugar: .5g

Protein: 1.5g

- Gluten-Free
- Dairy-Free
- Vegetarian
- Vegan
- Soy-Free

- Low-Sodium
- Low-Cal
- Low-Fat
- Low-Carb
- Low-Sugar

Cranberry Almond Coconut Snack Mix

Hope Comerford, Clinton Township, MI

Makes 12 servings

Prep. Time: 10 minutes ♨ Cooking Time: 2–3 hours ♨ Cooling Time: 1 hour ♨ Ideal slow cooker size: 6- or 7-qt.

5 cups gluten-free Cheerios

3 cups gluten-free Honey Nut Cheerios

1 cup gluten-free oats

1 cup dried cranberries

2 cups unsweetened shredded coconut

2 cups raw almonds, chopped

¼ cup melted coconut oil

¼ cup honey

½ tsp. cinnamon

½ tsp. salt

1 tsp. vanilla

1. Spray crock with non-stick spray.

2. Place the Cheerios, Honey Nut Cheerios, gluten-free oats, cranberries, coconut, and almonds into the crock.

3. In a bowl, whisk together the coconut oil, honey, cinnamon, salt, and vanilla. Pour this mixture over the cereal in the crock and gently stir with a rubber spatula until everything is evenly coated.

4. Place a paper towel under the lid, cover, and cook on low for 2–3 hours. Be sure to stir every 45 minutes or so to prevent burning.

5. When done cooking, pour mixture on parchment paper-lined baking sheet and let cool 1 hour. Once cooled, serve or store in an airtight container at room temperature for up to 3 weeks.

Calories: 380
Fat: 23g
Sodium: 200mg
Carbs: 42g
Sugar: 18g
Protein: 8.5g

- Gluten-Free
- Dairy-Free
- Vegetarian
- Soy-Free
- Low-Sodium
- Low-Cal

Gluten-Free Chex Mix

Hope Comerford, Clinton Township, MI

Makes 12 servings

Prep. Time: 8 minutes ⚜ *Cooking Time: 3 hours* ⚜ *Cooling Time: 1 hour* ⚜ *Ideal slow cooker size: 6- or 7-qt.*

3 cups gluten-free Rice Chex

3 cups gluten-free Corn Chex

3 cups gluten-free Cheerios

1 cup unsalted peanuts

⅓ cup coconut oil, melted

4 tsp. gluten-free Worcestershire sauce

1 tsp. sea salt

1 tsp. garlic powder

1 tsp. onion powder

1. Spray the crock with non-stick spray.

2. Place the Rice Chex, Corn Chex, Cheerios, and peanuts in the crock.

3. In a small bowl, whisk together the coconut oil, Worcestershire, sea salt, garlic powder, and onion powder. Pour this over the cereal in the crock and gently mix it with a rubber spatula until all cereal and peanuts are evenly coated.

4. Place a paper towel or thin dishcloth under the lid and cook on low for 3 hours, stirring once at the end of the first hour, once at the end of the second hour, and twice the last hour.

5. Spread the mixture onto parchment paper-lined baking sheets and let them cool for 1 hour.

6. Serve or keep in a sealed container at room temperature for up to 3 weeks.

Calories: 210
Fat: 13g
Sodium: 350mg
Carbs: 21g
Sugar: 3g
Protein: 5g

- Gluten-Free
- Dairy-Free
- Vegetarian
- Vegan

- Soy-Free
- Low-Cal
- Low-Sodium
- Low-Sugar

Rhonda's Apple Butter

Rhonda Burgoon, Collingswood, NJ

Makes 24 servings (2 Tbsp. each)
Prep. Time: 20 minutes ☙ Cooking Time: 12–14 hours ☙ Ideal slow cooker size: 3-qt.

4 lbs. apples
2 tsp. cinnamon
½ tsp. ground cloves

1. Peel, core, and slice apples. Place in slow cooker.

2. Cover. Cook on high 2–3 hours. Reduce to low and cook 8 hours. Apples should be a rich brown and be cooked down by half.

3. Stir in spices. Cook on high 2–3 hours with lid off. Stir until smooth.

4. Pour into freezer containers and freeze, or pour into sterilized jars and seal.

Calories: 40
Fat: 0g
Sodium: 0mg
Carbs: 10.5g
Sugar: 8g
Protein: 0g

- Gluten-Free
- Dairy-Free
- Soy-Free
- Low-Sugar
- No-Sodium
- Fat-Free
- Low-Cal
- Vegan
- Vegetarian
- Nut-Free

Pear Honey Butter

Becky Fixel, Grosse Pointe Farms, MI

Makes 45–50 servings

Prep. Time: 30 ❧ Cooking Time: 10 hours ❧ Ideal slow cooker size: 6½- or 7-qt.

10 lbs. ripened pears, peeled, cored, sliced

1 cup water

1 cup honey

1. Place your pear slices inside your slow cooker.

2. Add in the water and honey.

3. Cover and cook on low heat for 10 hours. You can stir if you want to but it's not necessary. When your pears are done, they will have darkened in color, but won't dry out through cooking.

4. Either use your blender and puree your softened pears in batches until it is done or use an immersion blender to make a smooth consistency.

Serving suggestion:
Serve on whole grain bread with cream cheese and top with cinnamon.

TIP
Freeze or can the extras in a water bath for 20 minutes.

Calories: 80
Fat: 0g
Sodium: 0mg
Carbs: 20g
Sugar: 15g
Protein: .5g

- Gluten-Free
- Dairy-Free
- Vegetarian
- Low-Cal
- Fat-Free
- No-Sodium

Soups, Stews & Chilies

Slow Cooker Tomato Soup

Becky Fixel, Grosse Pointe Farms, MI

Makes 8 servings

Prep. Time: 15 minutes ☙ Cooking Time: 6 hours ☙ Ideal slow cooker size: 6-qt.

6–8 cups chopped fresh tomatoes

1 medium onion, chopped

2 tsp. minced garlic

1 tsp. basil

½ tsp. pepper

½ tsp. sea salt

½ tsp. red pepper flakes

2 Tbsp. Massel chicken bouillon

1 cup water

¾ cup fat-free half-and-half

1. Combine your tomatoes, onion, spices, chicken bouillon, and 1 cup of water in your slow cooker.

2. Cover and cook on low for 6 hours.

3. Add in your ¾ cup fat-free half-and-half and combine all ingredients with an immersion blender. Serve hot.

Calories: 70
Fat: 0g
Sodium: 470mg
Carbs: 11g
Sugar: 6g
Protein: 1g

- Gluten-Free
- Vegetarian
- Soy-Free
- Nut-Free

- Low-Cal
- Fat-Free
- Low-Carb
- Low-Sugar

Chipotle Navy Bean Soup

Rebecca Weybright, Manheim, PA

Makes 6 servings

Prep. Time: 10 minutes ⚬ Cooking Time: 8 hours ⚬ Standing Time: 12 hours
⚬ Ideal slow cooker size: 5-qt.

1½ cups dried navy beans, soaked overnight

1 onion, chopped

1 dried chipotle chili, soaked 10–15 minutes in cold water

4 cups water

1–2 tsp. salt

2 cups canned tomatoes with juice

1. Drain soaked beans.

2. Add to slow cooker with onion, chili, and water.

3. Cover and cook on low for 8 hours until beans are creamy.

4. Add salt and tomatoes.

5. Use an immersion blender to puree soup.

Calories: 200
Fat: 1g
Sodium: 600mg
Carbs: 36g
Sugar: 5g
Protein: 12.5g

- Gluten-Free
- Dairy-Free
- Soy-Free
- Vegan
- Vegetarian

- Nut-Free
- Low-Cal
- Low-Fat
- Low-Sugar

Beans 'n Greens

Teri Sparks, Glen Burnie, MD

Makes 10 servings

Prep. Time: 30 minutes & Cooking Time: 6–8 hours & Ideal slow cooker size: 4- or 5-qt.

1 lb. dried 13-bean mix
5 cups gluten-free vegetable broth
¼ cup green onions, chopped
½ tsp. black pepper
2 Tbsp. dried parsley
1 yellow onion, coarsely chopped
3 cloves garlic, chopped
1 Tbsp. olive oil
6 cups fresh kale, torn in 2-inch pieces
Greek yogurt or sour cream, optional

1. Rinse and place beans in 4-quart slow cooker.

2. Add broth, green onions, pepper, and parsley.

3. In skillet, sauté yellow onion and garlic in oil. Add to beans in slow cooker.

4. Pile kale on top of bean mixture and cover with lid (crock will be very full).

5. Cook on high for 1 hour. Greens will have wilted some, so stir to combine all ingredients. Replace lid. Cook on low for 6-8 hours.

7. Top individual servings with dollops of Greek yogurt or sour cream if you wish.

Calories: 200
Fat: 2g
Sodium: 300mg
Carbs: 33g
Sugar: 3g
Protein: 11g

- Gluten-Free
- Vegan
- Vegetarian
- Low-Fat
- Soy-Free

- Nut-Free
- Low-Cal
- Low-Sodium
- Low-Sugar

Lentil Spinach Soup

Marilyn Widrick, Adams, NY

Makes 4–6 servings

Prep. Time: 10 minutes ⚜ *Cooking Time: 2½ hours* ⚜ *Ideal slow cooker size: 5-qt.*

1 Tbsp. olive oil

4 medium carrots, chopped

1 small onion, diced

1 tsp. ground cumin

14½-oz. can diced tomatoes

14½-oz. can gluten-free vegetable broth

1 cup dry lentils

2 cups water

¼ tsp. salt

⅛ tsp. pepper

5-oz. bag fresh spinach, chopped

1. Heat 1 Tbsp. olive oil in cooking pot. Add carrots and onion. Cook 8–10 minutes over medium heat.

2. Place carrots and onions in slow cooker. Add cumin, diced tomatoes, vegetable broth, dry lentils, water, salt, and pepper.

3. Cover and cook on low 2 hours.

4. Add spinach. Cook on low an additional 15–25 minutes.

Calories: 225
Fat: 3.5g
Sodium: 660mg
Carbs: 38.5g
Sugar: 8g
Protein: 12.5g

- Gluten-Free
- Dairy-Free
- Vegan
- Vegetarian
- Soy-Free

- Low-Fat
- Low-Cal
- Nut-Free
- Low-Sugar

Sweet Potato and Ginger Soup

Jenny Kempf, Bedminster, PA

Makes 4 servings

Prep. Time: 15 minutes ⚜ Cooking Time: 7–8 hours ⚜ Ideal slow cooker size: 6-qt.

I lb. sweet potatoes, peeled and cubed

2 tsp. coconut oil

2 tsp. chopped garlic

2 tsp. peeled, chopped ginger

2 cups gluten-free vegetable stock

I cup coconut milk

salt and pepper, to taste

2 Tbsp. fresh chopped cilantro

3 green onions, chopped

cashews, chopped, for garnish

1. Place sweet potatoes in slow cooker with coconut oil, garlic, ginger, vegetable stock, coconut milk, salt, and pepper.

2. Cover and cook on low for 7–8 hours, or until potatoes are tender.

3. Add cilantro and green onions.

4. Puree soup with hand blender or in stand blender. Pour into bowls or serving pot.

5. Sprinkle with cashews and serve.

Calories: 250
Fat: 14g
Sodium: 325mg
Carbs: 28g
Sugar: 7g
Protein: 2g

- Gluten-Free
- Dairy-Free
- Vegan
- Vegetarian

- Soy-Free
- Low-Cal
- Low-Sugar
- Low-Sodium

Vegetarian Split Pea Soup

Colleen Heatwole, Burton, MI

Makes 6 servings
Prep. Time: 30 minutes   ⚭   Cooking Time: 5–6 hours   ⚭   Ideal slow cooker size: 6-qt.

1 lb. split peas, sorted and rinsed

2 quarts gluten-free low-sodium vegetable broth

2 cups water

1 large onion, chopped

2 cloves garlic, minced

3 ribs celery, chopped

3 medium carrots, chopped finely

2 bay leaves

1 tsp. kosher salt

1 tsp. black pepper

1. Combine all ingredients and add to slow cooker.

2. Cover and cook on low 5–6 hours. Remove bay leaves and serve.

Serving suggestion:
If creamy texture is desired, blend with immersion blender.

TIP
If desired, add more salt after cooking, but note that this will increase sodium content.

Calories: 230
Fat: 0g
Sodium: 580mg
Carbs: 56g
Sugar: 7g
Protein: 20g

- Gluten-Free
- Dairy-Free
- Soy-Free
- Vegan
- Vegetarian

- Nut-Free
- Fat-Free
- Low-Cal
- Low-Sugar

Coconut-Curried Spinach Pea Soup

Allison Martin, Royal Oak, MI

Makes 12 servings

Prep. Time: 45 minutes ❧ Cooking Time: 7–8 hours ❧ Ideal slow cooker size: 5-qt.

5 cups water

2 tsp. salt

8 garlic cloves, peeled

4 cups sweet potatoes, peeled or unpeeled, and diced

1 Tbsp. coconut oil

4 cups chopped onions

1½ tsp. ginger

1½ tsp. turmeric

1½ tsp. cumin

1½ tsp. coriander

½ tsp. cinnamon

½ tsp. cardamom

¼–½ tsp. cayenne, according to your taste preference

black pepper, to taste

1½ Tbsp. lemon juice

3 cups frozen peas

4 cups torn fresh spinach

14-oz. can low-fat coconut milk

1. Combine all ingredients in your crock and mix well.

2. Cover and cook on low for 7–8 hours, or until the potatoes are tender when poked with a fork.

3. Purée soup with an immersion blender or a potato masher until as smooth as you like.

Serving suggestion:

Serve with an optional garnish of fresh cilantro and/or a dollop of non-fat plain Greek yogurt on top.

Calories: 125
Fat: 4g
Sodium: 465mg
Carbs: 22g
Sugar: 4g
Protein: 3g

- Gluten-Free
- Dairy-Free
- Soy-Free
- Nut-Free
- Vegan
- Vegetarian
- Low-Fat
- Low-Cal
- Low-Sugar

Butternut Squash Soup with Thai Gremalata

Andy Wagner, Quarryville, PA

Makes 4–6 servings

Prep. Time: 25 minutes   Cooking Time: 2–5 hours   Ideal slow cooker size: 3½- or 4-qt.

2 lbs. butternut squash, peeled and cut into 1-inch pieces

2 cups gluten-free vegetable broth

14-oz. can unsweetened coconut milk

¼ cup minced onions

1 Tbsp. brown sugar, packed

1 Tbsp. gluten-free soy sauce or Bragg's liquid aminos

½–1 tsp. crushed red pepper

2 Tbsp. lime juice

lime wedges, optional

Thai Gremolata:

½ cup chopped fresh basil or cilantro

½ cup chopped peanuts

1 Tbsp. finely shredded lime peel

1. In a 3½- or 4-quart slow cooker, stir together squash, broth, coconut milk, onions, brown sugar, soy sauce, and crushed red pepper.

2. Cover and cook on low for 4–5 hours or on high for 2–2½ hours.

3. Meanwhile, assemble the Thai Gremolata. Mix together basil, peanuts, and lime peel. Set aside.

4. Use an immersion or stand blender to carefully blend soup until completely smooth.

5. Stir in lime juice. Ladle into bowls and top with Thai Gremolata. If you wish, serve with lime wedges.

Calories: 285
Fat: 19g
Sodium: 600mg
Carbs: 31g
Sugar: 10.5g
Protein: 4g

- Gluten-Free
- Dairy-Free
- Vegan
- Vegetarian
- Low-Cal
- Low-Sugar

Potato Leek Soup

Melissa Paskvan, Novi, MI

Makes 4–6 servings
Prep. Time: 20 minutes ⚜ Cooking Time: 6 hours ⚜ Ideal slow cooker size: 6-qt.

3 large leeks, chopped (rinse leek well and include the tough tops)

5 medium Yukon Gold potatoes, chopped

2 cups gluten-free vegetable stock

2 cups water

2–3 bay leaves

½ head of cauliflower, broken up

3 stalks of celery, whole

¼ tsp pepper

salt to taste

1. Place all of the ingredients in the slow cooker and put the tough tops of the leeks on the top.

2. Cover and cook on low for 6 hours.

3. Remove tough leek tops, celery, and bay leaves. Either blend all the ingredients in a blender or use an immersion blender while in the crockpot and blend until very creamy. Salt to taste and add water if too thick for your liking.

Calories: 170
Fat: 0g
Sodium: 275mg
Carbs: 38g
Sugar: 5g
Protein: 6g

- Gluten-Free
- Dairy-Free
- Soy-Free
- Vegan
- Vegetarian

- Low-Cal
- Fat-Free
- Low-Sodium
- Low-Sugar

Serving suggestion:

Serve with scallions on top for a vegan option, with Monterey Jack cheese and scallions for a vegetarian option, or with bacon bits, scallions, and cheese for a meat eater option.

Chicken Tortilla Soup

Becky Fixel, Grosse Pointe Farms, MI

Makes 10–12 servings
Prep. Time: 5 minutes ⚜ Cooking Time: 7–8 hours ⚜ Ideal slow cooker size: 5-qt.

2 lbs. boneless skinless chicken breast

32 oz. gluten-free chicken stock

14 oz. verde sauce

10-oz. can diced tomatoes with lime juice

15-oz. can sweet corn, drained

1 Tbsp. minced garlic

1 small onion, diced

1 Tbsp. chili pepper

½ tsp. fresh ground pepper

½ tsp. salt

½ tsp. oregano

1 Tbsp. dried jalapeño slices

1. Add all ingredients to your slow cooker.

2. Cook on low for 7–8 hours.

3. Approximately 30 minutes before the end, remove your chicken and shred it into small pieces.

Serving suggestion:

Top with a dollop of non-fat plain Greek yogurt, shredded cheese, fresh jalapeños, or fresh cilantro.

Calories: 150
Fat: 3g
Sodium: 630mg
Carbs: 9g
Sugar: 4g
Protein: 20g

- Gluten-Free
- Dairy-Free
- Soy-Free
- Nut-Free

- Low-Cal
- Low-Fat
- Low-Carb
- Low-Sugar

Chicken Chickpea Tortilla Soup

Hope Comerford, Clinton Township, MI

Makes 4–6 servings
Prep. Time: 5 minutes 🌿 Cooking Time: 6 hours 🌿 Ideal slow cooker size: 4-qt.

2 boneless skinless chicken breasts

2 14½-oz. cans petite diced tomatoes

15-oz. can garbanzo beans (chickpeas), drained

6 cups gluten-free chicken stock

1 onion, chopped

4-oz. can diced green chilies

1 tsp. cilantro

3–4 fresh garlic cloves, minced

1 tsp. sea salt

1 tsp. pepper

1 tsp. cumin

1 tsp. paprika

1. Place all ingredients in slow cooker.

2. Cover and cook on low for 6 hours.

3. Use two forks to pull apart chicken into shreds.

Serving suggestion:

Serve with a small dollop of non-fat Greek yogurt, a little shredded cheddar, and some baked blue corn tortilla chips.

Calories: 420
Fat: 9g
Sodium: 1400mg
Carbs: 48.5g
Sugar: 18.5g
Protein: 38.5g

- Gluten-Free
- Dairy-Free
- Soy-Free

- Nut-Free
- Low-Fat
- High-Protein

White and Green Chili

Hope Comerford, Clinton Township, MI

Makes 6 servings

Prep. Time: 20 minutes   ♣   Cooking Time: 7–8 hours   ♣   Ideal slow cooker size: 4-qt.

1 lb. lean ground turkey, browned

1 cup chopped onion

2 15-oz. cans Great Northern beans, drained and rinsed

1 16-oz. jar salsa verde (green salsa)

2 cups gluten-free chicken broth

1 4-oz. can green chilies

1½ tsp. ground cumin

1 tsp. sea salt

¼ tsp. black pepper

2 Tbsp. fresh chopped cilantro

⅓ cup non-fat plain Greek yogurt, optional

1. Place all ingredients in crock except cilantro and Greek yogurt. Stir.

2. Cover and cook on low for 7–8 hours. Stir in cilantro.

Serving suggestion:

Serve each bowl of chili with a dollop of the Greek yogurt. Garnish with diced jalapeño peppers.

Calories: 325
Fat: 8g
Sodium: 1730mg
Carbs: 38g
Sugar: 6.5g
Protein: 26.5g

- Gluten-Free
- Soy-Free
- Nut-Free
- Low-Cal

- Low-Fat
- Low-Sugar
- High-Protein

Colorful Beef Stew

Hope Comerford, Clinton Township, MI

Makes 6 servings
Prep. Time: 20 minutes & Cooking Time: 8–9 hours & Ideal slow cooker size: 4-qt.

2 lbs. boneless beef chuck roast, trimmed of fat and cut into ¾-inch pieces

1 large red onion, chopped

2 cups gluten-free low-sodium beef broth

6-oz. can tomato paste

4 garlic cloves, minced

1 Tbsp. paprika

2 tsp. dried marjoram

½ tsp. black pepper

1 tsp. sea salt

1 red bell pepper, sliced

1 yellow bell pepper, sliced

1 orange bell pepper, sliced

1. Place all ingredients in the crock, except the sliced bell peppers, and stir.

2. Cover and cook on low for 8–9 hours. Stir in sliced bell peppers during the last 45 minutes of cooking time.

Calories: 443
Fat: 15g
Sodium: 180mg
Carbs: 15g
Sugar: 7g
Protein: 50g

- Gluten-Free
- Dairy-Free
- Soy-Free
- Nut-Free

- Low-Sodium
- Low-Sugar
- High-Protein

Enchilada Soup

Melissa Paskvan, Novi, MI

Makes 6–8 servings
Prep. Time: 5 minutes ⚶ Cooking Time: 6–8 hours ⚶ Ideal slow cooker size: 6-qt.

14.5-oz. can of diced tomatoes with green chilies or chipotles

12-oz. jar enchilada sauce

4 cups vegetable broth

1 small onion, chopped

3 cups tri-colored peppers, sliced

10-oz. pkg. frozen corn

1 cup water

½ cup uncooked quinoa

1. Add all ingredients to slow cooker.

2. Cover and cook on low for 6–8 hours.

Calories: 150
Fat: 2g
Sodium: 830mg
Carbs: 28g
Sugar: 7g
Protein: 4g

- Vegan
- Vegetarian
- Soy-Free
- Dairy-Free

- Nut-Free
- Low-Cal
- Low-Fat
- Low-Sugar

Chicken and Vegetable Soup

Hope Comerford, Clinton Township, MI

Makes 4–6 servings
Prep. Time: 15 minutes ⚜ Cooking Time: 7–8 hours ⚜ Ideal slow cooker size: 5-qt.

1 lb. boneless skinless chicken, cut into bite-sized pieces
2 celery ribs, diced
1 small yellow squash, diced
4 oz. sliced mushrooms
2 large carrots, diced
1 medium onion, chopped
2 Tbsp. garlic powder
1 Tbsp. onion powder
1 Tbsp. basil
½ tsp. no-salt seasoning
1 tsp. salt
black pepper to taste
32 oz. low-sodium chicken stock

1. Place the chicken, vegetables, and spices into the crock. Pour the chicken stock over the top.

2. Cover and cook on low for 7–8 hours, or until vegetables are tender.

Calories: 160
Fat: 2g
Sodium: 700mg
Carbs: 13g
Sugar: 5g
Protein: 23g

- Gluten-Free
- Dairy-Free
- Low-Carb
- Low-Sugar
- Low-Cal

- Soy-Free
- Nut-Free
- Low-Fat
- High Protein
- Paleo

Navy Bean and Ham Soup

Jennifer Freed, Rockingham, VA

Makes 6 servings
Prep. Time: overnight, or approximately 8 hours ⚭ *Cooking Time: 8–10 hours* ⚭
Ideal slow cooker size: 6½- or 7-qt.

6 cups water

5 cups dried navy beans, soaked overnight, drained, and rinsed

1 pound ham, cubed

15-oz. can corn, drained

4-oz. can mild diced green chilies, drained

1 onion, diced (optional)

salt and pepper to taste

1. Place all ingredients in slow cooker.

2. Cover and cook on low 8–10 hours, or until beans are tender.

Calories: 420
Fat: 5g
Sodium: 1200mg
Carbs: 103g
Sugar: 7g
Protein: 44g

- Gluten-Free
- Dairy-Free
- Soy-Free
- Egg-Free

- High Protein
- Low-Fat
- Low-Sugar

Jamaican Red Bean Stew

Andy Wagner, Quarryville, PA

Makes 6 servings
Prep. Time: 30 minutes ❧ Cooking Time: 6–8 hours ❧ Ideal slow cooker size: 4-qt.

1 Tbsp. extra-virgin olive oil

2 cloves garlic, minced

2 cups sliced carrots

3 green onions, chopped

1 sweet potato, diced

15-oz. can tomatoes, drained and diced

2 tsp. curry powder

½ tsp. dried thyme

¼ tsp. red pepper flakes

¼ tsp. ground allspice

salt and freshly ground black pepper, to taste

2 16-oz. cans dark red kidney beans, rinsed and drained

1 cup unsweetened coconut milk

1–2 cups unsalted gluten-free vegetable broth or water

1. Pour the oil into a 4-qt. slow cooker and set the cooker on high. Add the garlic and put the lid on the cooker while you prepare the rest of the ingredients.

2. Add carrots, green onions, sweet potato, and tomatoes to the cooker.

3. Stir in the curry powder, thyme, red pepper flakes, allspice, and salt and pepper to taste.

4. Add the beans, coconut milk, and broth.

5. Reduce heat to low, cover, and cook on low for 6–8 hours.

TIP

Use light coconut milk or reduce the amount to ½ cup for less saturated fat and calories. Reduce sodium in this recipe by thoroughly rinsing the canned beans and by using unsalted canned tomatoes.

Calories: 275
Fat: 9g
Sodium: 520mg
Carbs: 40g
Sugar: 10g
Protein: 10g

- Gluten-Free
- Vegetarian
- Vegan
- Dairy-Free

- Low-Fat
- Nut-Free
- Low-Cal

Chicken, Pumpkin, and Chickpea Stew

Andrea Maher, Dunedin, FL

Makes 6 servings
Prep. Time: 10 minutes ♣ Cooking Time: 6–8 hours ♣ Ideal slow cooker size: 5- or 6-qt.

24 oz. boneless skinless chicken, cut thin

3 cups canned pumpkin puree

2 cups chickpeas

3 cups mushrooms

1½ cups gluten-free low-sodium chicken broth

1½ cups plain non-fat Greek yogurt

salt to taste

pepper to taste

cinnamon to taste

red pepper and chili powder to taste, if desired

1. Add all ingredients to slow cooker.

2. Cook on high 3–4 hours or low 6–8.

TIP
This soup freezes well, so it's easy to freeze in portion-sized containers.

Calories: 275
Fat: 10g
Sodium: 230mg
Carbs: 28g
Sugar: 7g
Protein: 36g

- Gluten-Free
- Soy-Free
- Low-Sodium
- Low-Cal
- High-Protein
- Nut-Free
- Low-Sugar

Moroccan Spiced Stew

Melissa Paskvan, Novi, MI

Makes 6–8 servings

Prep. Time: 10 minutes ⚬ Cooking Time: 8 hours ⚬ Ideal slow cooker size: 5-qt.

3 cups canned chopped tomatoes

3 cups gluten-free chicken stock

1 lb. lamb (ground or stew-cut pieces)

1 medium onion, chopped

1/8 tsp. fresh grated ginger

1 1/2 tsp. cumin

3/4 tsp. cinnamon

3/4 tsp. turmeric

1/8 – 1/4 tsp. cayenne pepper

1/2 cup shredded or chopped carrots

3 cups chopped sweet potato

salt and pepper to taste

1. Place all ingredients in the crock and mix well to incorporate the spices.

2. Cover and cook on low for 8 hours.

Serving suggestion:

Top with Harissa for a zesty, warm flavor. Ladle this stew over brown rice or millet for a filling meal. Cook with 1/2 cup dried apricots or dates to impart a sweet taste.

TIP

If you really want to seal in the warm spices, add 1 Tbsp. olive oil to a pan and brown just the outsides of the lamb pieces and cook with onions and spices. Then add in about 1 cup of the chicken stock to deglaze the pan and pour all ingredients from the pan to the slow cooker and add the remaining ingredients. This can also be made vegan using quinoa and chickpeas for the protein and substituting with vegetable stock. I add 1/2 cup rinsed quinoa to the recipe and 1 can garbanzo beans (chickpeas).

Calories: 330
Fat: 19g
Sodium: 415mg
Carbs: 225.5g
Sugar: 9.5g
Protein: 16g

- Gluten-Free
- Dairy-Free
- Nut-Free
- Low-Cal
- Low-Sugar

Moroccan Beef Stew

Joyce Cox, Port Angeles, WA

Makes 4–6 servings
Prep. Time: 30 minutes ⚜ Cooking Time: 8–10 hours ⚜ Ideal slow cooker size: 4-qt.

3 Tbsp. olive oil, divided

2 cups thinly sliced onion

5 garlic cloves, minced

2-lb. beef chuck roast, cut into 2-inch cubes, seasoned with salt and pepper

15-oz. can diced tomatoes with juice

1 cup gluten-free low-sodium beef broth

1 Tbsp. honey

2 tsp. ground cumin

2 tsp. ground coriander

1 tsp. ground ginger

1 tsp. ground turmeric

1 cinnamon stick

1 bay leaf

black pepper to taste

1 cup pitted, chopped prunes

1. Heat 1½ Tbsp. olive oil in large frying pan and sauté onions until golden brown. Add garlic and cook 1 more minute. Transfer to slow cooker.

2. Heat remaining 1½ Tbsp. oil in pan. Sear beef cubes on all sides. Transfer to slow cooker.

3. Add rest of ingredients to slow cooker. Stir well.

4. Cover and cook on low for 8–10 hours. Remove cinnamon stick and bay leaf before serving.

Serving suggestion:

Serve over brown rice or quinoa.

Calories: 410
Fat: 19g
Sodium: 310mg
Carbs: 39g
Sugar: 22g
Protein: 18g

- Gluten-Free
- Dairy-Free
- Low-Sodium
- Nut-Free

Slow Cooker Beef Stew

Becky Fixel, Grosse Pointe Farms, MI

Makes 8–10 servings
Prep. Time: 30 minutes   Cooking Time: 6 hours   Ideal slow cooker size: 3-qt.

2 lbs. stew beef, cubed

¼ cup white rice flour

1½ tsp. salt

½ tsp. black pepper

32 oz. gluten-free organic beef broth

1 onion, diced

1 tsp. gluten-free Worcestershire sauce

1 bay leaf

1 tsp. paprika

4 carrots, sliced

3 potatoes, sliced thinly

1 stalk of celery, sliced

1. Place the meat in crock.

2. Mix the flour, salt, and pepper. Pour over the meat and mix well. Make sure to cover the meat with flour.

3. Add broth to the crock and stir well.

4. Add remaining ingredients and stir to mix well.

5. Cook on high for at least 5 hours, then on low for 1 hour. Remove bay leaf and serve.

Calories: 250
Fat: 4.5g
Sodium: 860mg
Carbs: 27g
Sugar: 1.5g
Protein: 26g

- Gluten-Free
- Dairy-Free
- Soy-Free
- Nut-Free
- Low-Fat
- Low-Sugar
- High-Protein

Black Bean Chili

Kenda Autumn, San Francisco, CA

Makes 6–8 servings

Prep. Time: 15 minutes ⚜ *Cooking Time: 8 hours* ⚜ *Ideal slow cooker size: 5-qt.*

1 Tbsp. olive oil

1 medium onion, chopped

1 tsp. ground cumin

1 tsp. ground coriander

1 Tbsp. chili powder

1 tsp. garam masala

16-oz. can black beans, rinsed and drained

14-oz. can diced tomatoes

1 sweet potato, cubed

2 cups cubed butternut squash

1 cup corn

1. Heat oil in saucepan. Brown onion, cumin, coriander, chili powder, and garam masala.

2. Transfer to slow cooker.

3. Add beans, tomatoes, sweet potato, butternut squash, and corn.

4. Cook on low 8 hours.

TIP
Use this recipe as a starting point for chili. I add other vegetables in step 3 that I have on hand, such as red bell pepper and mushrooms.

Calories: 240

Fat: 4g

Sodium: 300mg

Carbs: 46g

Sugar: 5g

Protein: 9g

- Gluten-Free
- Dairy-Free
- Soy-Free
- Vegan
- Vegetarian

- Low-Sodium
- Low-Fat
- Low-Cal
- Nut-Free
- Low-Sugar

Pumpkin Chili

Hope Comerford, Clinton Township, MI

Makes 8 servings
Prep. Time: 10 minutes ❧ Cooking Time: 7–8 hours ❧ Ideal slow cooker size: 6-qt.

16-oz. can kidney beans, drained and rinsed

16-oz. can black beans, drained and rinsed

1 large onion, chopped

½ green pepper, chopped

1 lb. ground turkey, browned

15-oz. can pumpkin puree

4 cups fresh chopped tomatoes

3 Tbsp. garlic powder

1 Tbsp. ancho chili powder

1 tsp. salt

2 tsp. cumin

¼ tsp. pepper

4 Tbsp. gluten-free beef bouillon granules

5 cups water

1. Place the kidney beans, black beans, onion, and pepper in the crock.

2. Crumble the ground turkey over the top and spoon the pumpkin puree on top of that.

3. Add in the remaining ingredients and stir.

4. Cover and cook on low for 7–8 hours.

Serving suggestion:

Garnish with pumpkin seeds.

Calories: 300
Fat: 7g
Sodium: 650mg
Carbs: 39.5g
Sugar: 6g
Protein: 22.5g

- Gluten-Free
- Soy-Free
- Dairy-Free
- Nut-Free

- Low-Sugar
- High-Protein
- Low-Cal
- Low-Fat

Southwestern Chili

Colleen Heatwole, Burton, MI

Makes 12 servings
Prep. Time: 30 minutes ⚶ Cooking Time: 6–8 hours ⚶ Ideal slow cooker size: 6- or 7-qt.

32-oz. can of whole tomatoes

15-oz. jar salsa

15-oz. can low-sodium chicken broth

1 cup barley

3 cups water

1 tsp. chili powder

1 tsp. ground cumin

15-oz. can black beans

15-oz. can whole kernel corn

3 cups cooked chicken, chopped

1 cup low-fat shredded cheddar cheese, optional

low fat sour cream, optional

1. Combine all ingredients in slow cooker except for optional cheese and sour cream.

2. Cover and cook on low for 6–8 hours.

3. Serve with optional cheese and sour cream on each bowl.

Calories: 300
Fat: 7g
Sodium: 650mg
Carbs: 39.5g
Sugar: 6g
Protein: 22.5g

- Low-Fat
- Egg-Free
- Nut-Free

- High-Protein
- Low-Cal
- Low-Sugar

Chipotle Chili

Janie Steele, Moore, OK

Makes 6–8 servings
Prep. Time: 30 minutes ❧ *Cooking Time: 3–6 hours* ❧ *Ideal slow cooker size: 3- or 4-qt.*

2 cloves garlic, chopped

1¼ lbs. boneless, skinless chicken thighs, cubed

1 lb. butternut squash, peeled and cubed

15-oz. can pinto beans, rinsed and drained

juice and zest of ½ orange

2–3 chipotle peppers in adobo sauce, minced

2 Tbsp. tomato paste

2 green onions, sliced, chopped

cilantro, optional

1. Combine garlic, chicken, squash, beans, orange juice, orange zest, peppers, and tomato paste in slow cooker.

2. Cook 3–4 hours on high or 5–6 hours on low until chicken is done.

3. Mash some of the stew with potato masher to make it thicker.

4. Stir in green onions and optional cilantro. Serve hot.

Calories: 210
Fat: 7g
Sodium: 260mg
Carbs: 20g
Sugar: 3g
Protein: 22g

- Gluten-Free
- Dairy-Free
- Soy-Free
- Low-Fat

- Low-Sugar
- High-Protein
- Low-Cal
- Low-Sodium

Main Dishes

Asian Style Chicken with Pineapple

Andrea Maher, Dunedin, FL

Makes 6 servings

Prep. Time: 10 minutes & Cooking Time: 6–8 hours & Ideal slow cooker size: 5- or 6-qt.

24 oz. boneless skinless chicken breast cut into bite size pieces

3 cups pineapple, cubed

¼ cup Bragg's liquid aminos

1 Tbsp. brown sugar

½ cup chopped onion or 2 Tbsp. onion powder

1 cup low-sodium gluten-free chicken broth or stock

½ tsp. ground ginger

2 16-oz. bags frozen Szechuan mixed veggies or any mixed veggies

1. Add all ingredients except for frozen veggies to the slow cooker.

2. Cover and cook on high 3–4 hours or low 6–8 hours.

3. Add frozen veggies in the last 1–2 hours.

Calories: 280
Fat: 2g
Sodium: 830mg
Carbs: 38g
Sugar: 16g
Protein: 32g

- Low-Carb
- Gluten-Free
- Dairy-Free

- High-Protein
- Low-Cal
- Low-Fat

Juicy Orange Chicken

Andrea Maher, Dunedin, FL

Makes 6 servings
Prep. Time: 10 minutes ❧ Cooking Time: 6–8 hours ❧ Ideal slow cooker size: 5- or 6-qt.

18–24 oz. boneless, skinless chicken breast, cut into small pieces
1 cup orange juice, no additives
¼ cup honey
6 small oranges, peeled and sliced
¼ cup Bragg's liquid aminos
6 cups broccoli slaw

1. Add all the ingredients to the slow cooker except the broccoli slaw.

2. Cover and cook on high 3–4 hours or low 6–8 hours.

3. Divide mixture between 6 mason jars.

4. Add 1 cup broccoli slaw to each mason jar.

5. Pour into a bowl when you're ready to eat!

Calories: 240
Fat: 2g
Sodium: 730mg
Carbs: 33g
Sugar: 25g
Protein: 26g

- High-Protein
- Gluten-Free
- Dairy-Free

- Low-Cal
- Low-Fat

Italian Crockpot Chicken

Andrea Maher, Dunedin, FL

Makes 6 servings
Prep. Time: 5 minutes ⚬ Cooking Time: 6–8 hours ⚬ Ideal slow cooker size: 6-qt.

24 oz. boneless skinless chicken breast, cut into small pieces

3 cups garbanzo beans

16-oz. bag frozen spinach

2 cups mushrooms

2 Tbsp. Mrs. Dash Italian seasoning

1 cup low-sodium gluten-free chicken broth

1. Add all ingredients to the slow cooker.

2. Cover and cook on low for 6–8 hours or high for 3–4 hours.

Calories: 280
Fat: 4g
Sodium: 270mg
Carbs: 25g
Sugar: 4g
Protein: 34g

- High-Protein
- Gluten-Free
- Dairy-Free
- Low-Sodium
- Low-Cal
- Low-Fat
- Low-Sugar

Garlic and Lemon Chicken

Hope Comerford, Clinton Township, MI

Makes 5 servings
Prep. Time: 5 minutes ⚬ *Cooking Time: 5–6 hours* ⚬ *Ideal slow cooker size: 3- or 5-qt.*

4–5 lbs. boneless skinless chicken breasts or thighs

½ cup minced shallots

½ cup olive oil

¼ cup lemon juice

I Tbsp. garlic paste (or use I medium clove garlic, minced)

I Tbsp. no-salt seasoning

⅛ tsp. pepper

1. Place chicken in slow cooker.

2. In a small bowl, mix the remaining ingredients. Pour this mixture over the chicken in the crock.

3. Cover and cook on low for 5–6 hours.

Calories: 450
Fat: 9g
Sodium: 260mg
Carbs: 3g
Sugar: 0g
Protein: 87g

- Gluten-Free
- Dairy-Free
- Low-Sodium
- High-Protein

- Low-Fat
- Sugar-Free
- Low-Carb
- Paleo

Easy Enchilada Shredded Chicken

Hope Comerford, Clinton Township, MI

Makes 10–14 servings

Prep. Time: 5 minutes ⚭ Cooking Time: 5–6 hours ⚭ Ideal slow cooker size: 3- or 5-qt.

5–6 lbs. boneless skinless chicken breast

14.5-oz. can petite diced tomatoes

1 medium onion, chopped

8 oz. red enchilada sauce

½ tsp. salt

½ tsp. chili powder

½ tsp. basil

½ tsp. garlic powder

¼ tsp. pepper

1. Place chicken in the crock.

2. Add in the remaining ingredients.

3. Cover and cook on low for 5–6 hours.

4. Remove chicken and shred it between two forks. Place the shredded chicken back in the crock and stir to mix in the juices.

Serving suggestion:

Serve over salad, brown rice, quinoa, sweet potatoes, nachos, or soft shell corn tacos. Add a dollop of yogurt and a sprinkle of fresh cilantro.

Calories: 240
Fat: 5g
Sodium: 340mg
Carbs: 4g
Sugar: 2g
Protein: 44g

- Gluten-Free
- Dairy-Free
- High-Protein
- Low-Sodium
- Low-Cal
- Low-Fat
- Low-Sugar

Chicken Dijon Dinner

Barbara Stutzman, Crossville, TN

Makes 4–6 servings
Prep. Time: 20 minutes ⚜ Cooking Time: 4 hours ⚜ Ideal slow cooker size: 6-qt.

2 lbs. boneless, skinless chicken thighs

2 garlic cloves, minced

1 Tbsp. olive oil

6 Tbsp. white wine vinegar

4 Tbsp. gluten-free soy sauce or Bragg's liquid aminos

4 Tbsp. Dijon mustard

1 lb. sliced mushrooms

1. Grease slow cooker crock.

2. Place thighs in the crock. If you need to add a second layer, stagger the pieces so they don't directly overlap each other.

3. Stir together garlic, oil, vinegar, soy sauce, and mustard until well mixed.

4. Gently stir in mushrooms.

5. Spoon sauce into crock, making sure to cover all thighs with some of the sauce.

6. Cover and cook on low for 4 hours, or until instant-read thermometer registers 160°F when stuck in center of chicken.

7. Serve chicken topped with sauce.

Calories: 325
Fat: 19g
Sodium: 1180mg
Carbs: 5g
Sugar: 2g
Protein: 44g

- Gluten-Free
- Nut-Free
- High-Protein
- Low-Cal

- Low-Carb
- Low-Sugar
- Paleo

Garlic Mushroom Thighs

Elaine Vigoda, Rochester, NY

Makes 6 servings
Prep. Time: 15 minutes ♣ Cooking Time: 4 hours ♣ Ideal slow cooker size: 5-qt.

6 boneless skinless chicken thighs

3 Tbsp. gluten-free flour

8–10 garlic cloves, peeled and very lightly crushed

1 Tbsp. olive oil

¾ lb. fresh mushrooms, any combination of varieties, cut into bite-sized pieces

⅓ cup balsamic vinegar

1¼ cups gluten-free chicken broth or stock

1–2 bay leaves

½ tsp. dried thyme or 4 sprigs fresh thyme

2 tsp. apricot preserves (low-sugar or no sugar added preferred)

Serving suggestion:

Serve over cooked spaghetti squash.

Calories: 340
Fat: 18g
Sodium: 180mg
Carbs: 10g
Sugar: 5g
Protein: 34g

- Gluten-Free
- Dairy-Free
- Soy-Free
- Low-Sodium
- Low-Cal
- High-Protein
- Low-Sugar

1. Grease interior of slow cooker.

2. Place gluten-free flour in a strong plastic bag without any holes. Once by one, put each thigh in bag, hold the bag shut, and shake it to flour the thigh fully.

3. Place thighs in the crock. If you need to make a second layer, stagger the pieces so they don't directly overlap.

4. If you have time, sauté the garlic in oil in skillet just until it begins to brown. Otherwise, use raw.

5. Sprinkle garlic over thighs, including those on bottom layer.

6. Scatter cut-up mushrooms over thighs too, remembering those on the bottom layer.

7. Mix remaining ingredients together in a bowl, stirring to break up the preserves.

8. When well mixed, pour into the cooker along the edges so you don't wash the vegetables off the chicken pieces.

9. Cover and cook on low for 4 hours, or until an instant read thermometer registers 160–165°F when stuck into the thighs.

10. Serve meat topped with vegetables with sauce spooned over.

Southwestern Shredded Chicken

Hope Comerford, Clinton Township, MI

Makes 4 servings

Prep. Time: 8–10 minutes & Cooking Time: 5–6 hours & Ideal slow cooker size: 3-qt.

1½ lbs. boneless skinless chicken breast

1 Tbsp. chili powder

2 tsp. garlic powder

1 tsp. cumin

1 tsp. onion powder

½ tsp. kosher salt

¼ tsp. pepper

1 medium onion, chopped

14.5-oz. can diced tomatoes

4-oz. can diced green chilies

½ cup non-fat Greek yogurt

optional toppings: lettuce, shredded cheese, Greek yogurt, and salsa

1. Place the chicken in the slow cooker.

2. Mix together the chili powder, garlic powder, cumin, onion powder, kosher salt, and pepper. Sprinkle this over both sides of the chicken.

3. Sprinkle the onions over the top of the chicken and pour the can of diced tomatoes and green chilies over the top.

4. Cover and cook on low for 5–6 hours.

5. Turn your slow cooker to warm. Remove the chicken and shred it between 2 forks.

6. Slowly whisk in the non-fat Greek yogurt with the juices in the crock. Replace the chicken in the crock and stir to mix in the juices.

Serving suggestion:

Serve this over brown rice or quinoa topped with some shredded lettuce, shredded cheese, and fresh salsa.

Calories: 250
Fat: 4g
Sodium: 600mg
Carbs: 13g
Sugar: 6g
Protein: 41g

- Gluten-Free
- Low-Fat
- Low-Cal
- High-Protein
- Low-Sugar

Simple Savory Chicken

Hope Comerford, Clinton Township, MI

Makes 4–6 servings
Prep. Time: 5–8 minutes ☙ Cooking Time: 7–8 hours ☙ Ideal slow cooker size: 3-qt.

2 lbs. skinless chicken leg quarters

¼ cup chopped onion

2 cloves garlic, minced

1 tsp. basil

1 tsp. dill

½ tsp. salt

¼ tsp. black pepper

1 cup water

2 Tbsp. apple cider vinegar

1. Place the chicken in the crock. Sprinkle with the onions and garlic.

2. In a bowl, mix together the basil, dill, salt, and pepper. Sprinkle this evenly over the chicken.

3. Pour in the water and apple cider vinegar around the chicken, being careful not to wash off the spices.

4. Cover and cook on low for 7–8 hours.

Serving suggestion:

Serve with the Cauliflower Cassoulet (page 231) and Aunt Twila's Beans (page 273).

Calories: 225
Fat: 7.5g
Sodium: 410mg
Carbs: 1.5g
Sugar: .5g
Protein: 35g

- Gluten-Free
- Dairy-Free
- Low-Cal
- High-Protein

- Low-Fat
- Low-Sugar
- Low-Carb
- Paleo

Buffalo Chicken Meatballs

Hope Comerford, Clinton Township, MI

Makes 6 servings
Prep. Time: 20–30 minutes & Cooking Time: 6 hours & Ideal slow cooker size: 5- or 6-qt.

1½ lbs. ground chicken

¾ cup gluten-free hot sauce of your choice, divided

2 Tbsp. dry minced onion

2 Tbsp. garlic powder

¼ tsp. pepper

1 egg

1 cup gluten-free panko bread crumbs

1½–2 Tbsp. coconut oil

2 tsp. gluten-free chicken bouillon granules

1 cup water

2 cups non-fat plain Greek yogurt

2 Tbsp. cornstarch

1. In a bowl, combine the ground chicken, ½ cup hot sauce, minced onion, garlic powder, pepper, egg, and gluten-free panko bread crumbs.

2. Heat the coconut oil in a large skillet over medium-high heat.

3. Roll the chicken mixture into 1½–2-inch balls. Place them in the skillet, turning them regularly so they're seared on each side.

4. Place the seared meatballs into your crock. Sprinkle them with the chicken bouillon granules and pour in the water.

5. Cover and cook on low for 6 hours.

6. Remove the meatballs in a covered dish to keep them warm.

7. In a bowl, stir together the Greek yogurt, corn starch, and remaining ¼ cup of hot sauce. Gently whisk this back into your crock with the juices.

8. You can either place your browned meatballs back into the sauce to coat them, or you can serve the meatballs with the sauce spooned over the top.

Serving suggestion:

Serve meatballs over browned rice with a fresh salad on the side. If desired, add more hot sauce to taste.

Calories: 420
Fat: 14g
Sodium: 650mg
Carbs: 44g
Sugar: 3g
Protein: 29g

- Gluten-Free
- Low-Fat
- Low-Cal
- High-Protein
- Low-Sugar

Chicken Chow Mein

Hope Comerford, Clinton Township, MI

Makes 6 servings

Prep. Time: 15–20 minutes ❧ Cooking Time: 6½–7½ hours ❧ Ideal slow cooker size: 3- or 4-qt.

2–3 large boneless skinless chicken breasts

2 cups water

2 medium onions, halved and sliced into half rings

2–3 cups chopped celery

1 tsp. kosher salt

¼ tsp. pepper

2 tsp. quick-cooking tapioca

¼ cup low sodium gluten-free soy sauce or Bragg's liquid aminos

¼ cup brown sugar

16-oz. can baby corn, drained

6.5-oz. can bamboo shoots, drained

1 cup bean sprouts

1 red bell pepper, chopped into slivers

1 carrot, chopped into thin matchsticks

1. Place the chicken breasts in the crock with the water, onions, celery, salt, and pepper.

2. Cover and cook on low for 5–6 hours.

3. While the chicken is cooking, in a small bowl mix together the tapioca, gluten-free soy sauce, and brown sugar.

4. Remove the chicken and shred it between 2 forks.

5. Mix the sauce you just made with the juices in the slow cooker. Add the chicken back in and all the remaining veggies. Stir.

6. Cook on low an additional 1½ hours.

Serving suggestion:

Serve over gluten-free Chinese or Thai rice noodles.

Calories: 180
Fat: 2g
Sodium: 1200mg
Carbs: 26g
Sugar: 15g
Protein: 18g

- Gluten-Free
- Dairy-Free
- Low-Fat
- Low-Cal

Chicken Mole

Bernadette Veenstra, Grand Rapids, MI

Makes 8 servings
Prep. Time: 30 minutes ⚓ Cooking Time: 4–5 hours ⚓ Ideal slow cooker size: 6-qt.

1 Tbsp. olive oil

8–10 chicken thighs, skinned and lightly salted and peppered

1 large onion

4–6 garlic cloves, minced

4 tsp. chili powder

4 tsp. unsweetened cocoa powder

¼ tsp. cinnamon

2½ cups gluten-free chicken broth or stock

2 Tbsp. natural creamy peanut butter

2 Tbsp. tomato paste

½ cup dark raisins

4 cups cooked brown rice

½ cup loosely packed cilantro leaves

lime wedges

1. Heat olive oil in a large skillet. In several batches, brown all sides of chicken (about 10 minutes total).

2. Place chicken in bottom of slow cooker lightly coated with cooking spray. Discard all but 1 Tbsp. of pan drippings.

3. Heat pan drippings or oil in same skillet. Add onion and cook, stirring until softened (about 5 minutes). Add garlic, chili powder, cocoa powder, and cinnamon to skillet and cook, stirring 1 minute.

4. Stir in broth, peanut butter, and tomato paste.

5. Pour sauce over chicken in slow cooker.

6. Cook on low for 4–5 hours, or until chicken registers 165°F on meat thermometer.

7. Serve over cooked brown rice and garnish with cilantro and lime wedges.

Calories: 330
Fat: 12g
Sodium: 275mg
Carbs: 35g
Sugar: 8g
Protein: 40g

- Gluten-Free
- Dairy-Free
- Soy-Free
- High-Protein

- Low-Cal
- Low-Sodium
- Low-Sugar

Honey Balsamic Chicken

Hope Comerford, Clinton Township, MI

Makes 4–6 servings

Prep. Time: 5 minutes ☙ Cooking Time: 7–8 hours ☙ Ideal slow cooker size: 5- or 6-qt.

4 cups chopped red potatoes

1½ tsp. kosher salt, divided

1 tsp. pepper, divided

8–10 boneless skinless chicken thighs

1 cup sliced red onion

1 pint cherry tomatoes

½ cup balsamic vinegar

¼ cup honey

2 Tbsp. olive oil

¼ tsp. red pepper flakes

½ tsp. dried thyme

½ tsp. dried rosemary

3 cloves garlic, minced

3 cups green beans

1. Spray crock with non-stick cooking spray.

2. Place potatoes in bottom of crock. Sprinkle with ½ tsp. of salt and ½ tsp. pepper.

3. Place chicken on top of potatoes and pour cherry tomatoes over the top.

4. Mix together the balsamic vinegar, honey, olive oil, 1 tsp. salt, remaining ½ tsp. pepper, red pepper flakes, thyme, rosemary, and garlic. Pour this mixture over the chicken, tomatoes, and potatoes.

5. Cook on low for 7–8 hours, or until potatoes are tender.

6. 20–30 minutes before serving, add the green beans on top.

Serving suggestion:

To serve, spoon the juices from the crock over the chicken and vegetables. Serve alongside "Baked" Sweet Potatoes (page 261).

Calories: 285
Fat: 10g
Sodium: 540mg
Carbs: 33g
Sugar: 15g
Protein: 39g

- Gluten-Free
- Dairy-Free
- High-Protein
- Low-Cal
- Low-Fat

Turkey "Spaghetti" Quinoa

Hope Comerford, Clinton Township, MI

Makes 8–10 servings
Prep. Time: 10–15 minutes ❧ Cooking Time: 5 hours ❧ Ideal slow cooker size: 5- or 6-qt.

2 lbs. lean ground turkey

½ tsp. salt

⅛ tsp. pepper

1 tsp. garlic powder

1 tsp. onion powder

1 cup quinoa

1 cup chopped onion

1 cup shredded mozzarella cheese (for dairy-free, substitute with dairy-free cheese or leave out)

4 cups tomato sauce

2 cups water

1. Brown turkey with the salt, pepper, garlic powder, and onion powder.

2. Spray crock with non-stick spray.

3. Place ground turkey in bottom of crock. Top with quinoa, onion, and shredded mozzarella.

4. Pour tomato sauce and water into crock. Stir so everything is mixed.

5. Cover and cook on low for 5 hours.

Calories: 300
Fat: 12.5g
Sodium: 800mg
Carbs: 20.5g
Sugar: 5g
Protein: 26g

- Gluten-Free
- Dairy-Free
- Soy-Free
- Nut-Free

- Low-Cal
- Low-Sugar
- High-Protein

Turkey with Mushroom Sauce

Judi Manos, West Islip, NY

Makes 12 servings

Prep. Time: 25 minutes & Cooking Time: 7–8 hours & Ideal slow cooker size: 6-qt.

1 large boneless skinless turkey breast, halved

2 Tbsp. melted coconut oil

2 Tbsp. dried parsley

½ tsp. dried oregano

½ tsp. kosher salt

¼ tsp. black pepper

½ cup white wine

1 cup fresh mushrooms, sliced

2 Tbsp. cornstarch

¼ cup cold water

1. Place turkey in slow cooker. Brush with coconut oil.

2. Mix together parsley, oregano, salt, pepper, and wine. Pour over turkey.

3. Top with mushrooms.

4. Cover and cook on low for 7–8 hours or just until turkey is tender.

5. Remove turkey and keep warm.

6. Skim any fat from cooking juices.

7. In a saucepan over low heat combine cornstarch and water and mix until smooth. Gradually add cooking juices from the crock. Bring to a boil. Cook and stir 2 minutes until thickened.

8. Slice turkey and serve with sauce.

Calories: 200
Fat: 4.5g
Sodium: 265mg
Carbs: 2g
Sugar: .5g
Protein: 35g

- Gluten-Free
- Low-Fat
- Dairy-Free
- Low-Cal

- Low-Sodium
- Low-Carb
- Low-Sugar
- High-Protein

Thyme and Garlic Turkey Breast

Hope Comerford, Clinton Township, MI

Makes 6–8 servings
Prep. Time: 10 minutes ⚶ Cooking Time: 7–8 hours ⚶ Ideal slow cooker size: 6- or 7-qt.

4 lb. bone-in turkey breast, giblets removed if there are any, skin removed, washed and patted dry

¼ cup olive oil

1 Tbsp. balsamic vinegar

1 Tbsp. water

1 orange, juiced

6 cloves garlic, minced

1½ tsp. dried thyme

1 tsp. onion powder

1 tsp. kosher salt

1. Place turkey breast in crock.

2. Mix together the remaining ingredients and pour over the turkey breast. Rub it in on all sides with clean hands.

3. Cover and cook on low for 7–8 hours.

Calories: 360
Fat: 11.5g
Sodium: 610mg
Carbs: 3.5g
Sugar: 1.5g
Protein: 58g

- Gluten-Free
- Dairy-Free
- Soy-Free
- Nut-Free
- Low-Sugar

- High-Protein
- Low-Cal
- Low-Fat
- Low-Carb
- Paleo

Zucchini-Vegetable Pot

Edwina Stoltzfus, Narvon, PA

Makes 6 servings
Prep. Time: 40 minutes & Cooking Time: 3–4 hours & Ideal slow cooker size: 3½- or 4-qt.

1 lb. lean ground turkey
2 cups diced zucchini
2 ribs celery, chopped
¼ cup chopped green bell peppers
1 large onion, chopped
2 large tomatoes, chopped
¼ cup brown rice, uncooked
¾ tsp. sea salt
¼ tsp. garlic powder
⅛ tsp. nutmeg
¼ tsp. black pepper
1 tsp. gluten-free Worcestershire sauce

1. Brown turkey in non-stick skillet.

2. Meanwhile, place vegetables in slow cooker. Top with rice and ground turkey.

3. Sprinkle seasonings over top and add Worcestershire sauce.

4. Cover and cook on high for 3–4 hours.

Calories: 175
Fat: 7g
Sodium: 370mg
Carbs: 13g
Sugar: 4g
Protein: 16.5g

- Gluten-Free
- Dairy-Free
- Low-Cal
- Low-Fat

- Low-Sugar
- Low-Cal
- Low-Carb

Moist and Tender Turkey Breast

Marlene Weaver, Lititz, PA

Makes 12 servings

Prep. Time: 10 minutes ⚘ Cooking Time: 4–6 hours ⚘ Ideal slow cooker size: 6- or 7-qt.

1 bone-in turkey breast (6–7 lbs.)

4 fresh rosemary sprigs

4 garlic cloves, peeled

1 Tbsp. brown sugar

½ tsp. coarsely ground pepper

¼ tsp. salt

1. Place turkey in a crock and place rosemary and garlic around it.

2. Combine the brown sugar, pepper, and salt; sprinkle over turkey.

3. Cover and cook on low for 4–6 hours or until turkey is tender.

Serving suggestion:

Serve alongside Garden Chips (page 255) and Honey Roasted Parsnips, Sweet Potatoes, and Apples (page 267).

Calories: 300
Fat: 13.25g
Sodium: 160mg
Carbs: 1.5g
Sugar: 1g
Protein: 41.5g

- Gluten-Free
- Dairy-Free
- Low-Fat
- Low-Sodium
- High-Protein

Spaghetti with Meat Sauce

Becky Fixel, Grosse Pointe Farms, MI

Makes 6–8 servings

Prep. Time: 20 minutes   Cooking Time: 8 hours   Ideal slow cooker size: 7-qt.

2 Tbsp. olive oil

28-oz. can crushed tomatoes

28-oz. can tomato sauce

15-oz. can Italian stewed tomatoes

6-oz. can tomato paste

2–3 Tbsp. basil

2 Tbsp. oregano

2 Tbsp. brown sugar

2 Tbsp. garlic paste (or 2 medium cloves, peeled and minced)

2 lbs. extra-lean ground sirloin or lean ground turkey

1. Pour olive oil in the crock. Use a paper towel to rub it all around the inside.

2. Add all ingredients except ground sirloin or turkey. Stir together and put slow cooker on low.

3. In a large skillet, brown your ground sirloin, and drain off any extra grease. Add this to your slow cooker.

4. Cook on low for 8 hours.

Serving suggestion:

Serve over your favorite gluten-free pasta.

Calories: 370
Fat: 17g
Sodium: 360mg
Carbs: 28.5g
Sugar: 19g
Protein: 29.5g

- Gluten-Free
- Dairy-Free
- Low-Cal
- Low-Fat
- Low-Sodium
- Low-Carb
- Low-Sugar
- Nut-Free
- Soy-Free

Four-Pepper Steak

Renee Hankins, Narvon, PA

Makes 14 servings
Prep. Time: 30 minutes ❧ Cooking Time: 5–8 hours ❧ Ideal slow cooker size: 4- or 5-qt.

1 yellow pepper, sliced into ¼-inch thick pieces

1 red pepper, sliced into ¼-inch thick pieces

1 orange pepper, sliced into ¼-inch thick pieces

1 green pepper, sliced into ¼-inch thick pieces

2 garlic cloves, sliced

2 large onions, sliced

1 tsp. ground cumin

½ tsp. dried oregano

1 bay leaf

3 lb. flank steak, cut in ¼–½-inch thick slices across the grain

salt to taste

2 14.5-oz. cans low-sodium diced tomatoes in juice

jalapeño chilies, sliced, optional

1. Place sliced bell peppers, garlic, onions, cumin, oregano, and bay leaf in slow cooker. Stir gently to mix.

2. Put steak slices on top of vegetable mixture. Season with salt.

3. Spoon tomatoes with juice over top. Sprinkle with jalapeño pepper slices if you wish. Do not stir.

4. Cover and cook on low 5–8 hours, depending on your slow cooker. Check after 5 hours to see if meat is tender. If not, continue cooking until tender but not dry. Remove bay leaf and serve.

Calories: 170
Fat: 5g
Sodium: 60mg
Carbs: 9g
Sugar: 4.5g
Protein: 22.5g

- Gluten-Free
- Dairy-Free
- Low-Sodium
- Low-Fat
- Low-Cal
- Low-Carb
- Low-Sugar
- High-Protein
- Paleo

Hungarian Beef with Paprika

Maureen Csikasz, Wakefield, MA

Makes 9 servings
Prep. Time: 15 minutes   ⚶   Cooking Time: 3–6 hours   ⚶   Ideal slow cooker size: oval 5- or 6-qt.

3 lb. boneless chuck roast

2–3 medium onions, coarsely chopped

5 Tbsp. sweet paprika

¾ tsp. salt

¼ tsp. black pepper

½ tsp. caraway seeds

1 clove garlic, chopped

½ green bell pepper, sliced

¼ cup water

½ cup non-fat plain Greek yogurt

fresh parsley

1. Grease interior of slow cooker crock.

2. Place roast in crock.

3. In a good-sized bowl, mix all ingredients together, except non-fat plain Greek yogurt and parsley.

4. Spoon evenly over roast.

5. Cover. Cook on high 3–4 hours, or on low 5–6 hours, or until instant-read meat thermometer registers 140–145°F when stuck in center of meat.

6. When finished cooking, use sturdy tongs or 2 metal spatulas to lift meat to cutting board. Cover with foil to keep warm. Let stand 10–15 minutes.

7. Cut into chunks or slices.

8. Just before serving, dollop with non-fat plain Greek yogurt. Garnish with fresh parsley.

Calories: 250
Fat: 10.5g
Sodium: 320mg
Carbs: 6.5g
Sugar: 2.5g
Protein: 34.5g

- Low-Carb
- High-Protein
- Gluten-Free
- Low-Cal

- Low-Fat
- Low-Sodium
- Low-Sugar

Spicy Beef Roast

Karen Ceneviva, Seymour, CT

Makes 10 servings
Prep. Time: 15–20 minutes ❧ Cooking Time: 3–8 hours ❧ Ideal slow cooker size: 4- or 5-qt.

3 lb. eye of round roast, trimmed of fat

1–2 Tbsp. cracked black peppercorns

2 cloves garlic, minced

3 Tbsp. balsamic vinegar

¼ cup gluten-free reduced-sodium soy sauce or Bragg's liquid aminos

2 Tbsp. gluten-free Worcestershire sauce

2 tsp. dry mustard

1. Rub cracked pepper and garlic onto roast. Put roast in slow cooker.

2. Make several shallow slits in top of meat.

3. In a small bowl, combine remaining ingredients. Spoon over meat.

4. Cover and cook on low for 6–8 hours, or on high for 3–4 hours, just until meat is tender, but not dry.

Calories: 240
Fat: 6g
Sodium: 530mg
Carbs: 2g
Sugar: 1g
Protein: 41.5g

- Gluten-Free
- Dairy-Free
- Nut-Free
- Low-Cal
- Low-Fat

- High-Protein
- Low-Carb
- Low-Sugar
- High-Protein
- Paleo

Low-Fat Slow Cooker Roast

Charlotte Shaffer, East Earl, PA

Makes 10 servings

Prep. Time: 15 minutes   ❀   Cooking Time: 3–8 hours   ❀   Ideal slow cooker size: 6-qt.

3 lb. boneless beef roast

4 carrots, peeled and cut into 2-inch pieces

4 potatoes, cut into quarters

2 onions, quartered

I cup gluten-free, low-sodium beef broth or stock

I tsp. garlic powder

I tsp. Mrs. Dash seasoning

½ tsp. salt

½ tsp. black pepper

1. Place roast in slow cooker.

2. Add carrots around edges, pushing them down so they reach the bottom of the crock.

3. Add potatoes and onions.

4. Mix together broth and seasonings and pour over roast.

5. Cover and cook on low for 6–8 hours, or on high for 3–4 hours.

Calories: 340
Fat: 12g
Sodium: 275mg
Carbs: 20g
Sugar: 3g
Protein: 39g

- Gluten-Free
- Dairy-Free
- Low-Fat
- Low-Cal
- Nut-Free
- Soy-Free
- Low-Sodium
- Low-Sugar
- High-Protein

Espresso Braised Beef

Dena Mell-Dorchy, Royal Oak, MI

Makes 6 servings

Prep. Time: 25 minutes ⚬ *Cooking Time: 8–9 hours* ⚬ *Ideal slow cooker size: 3- or 4-qt.*

1 large onion, cut into wedges

3 medium carrots, cut into ½-inch pieces

1 medium turnip, cut into 1-inch pieces

3 celery stalks, cut into 1-inch pieces

1½ lbs. boneless beef chuck, cut into 1-inch pieces

⅔ cup gluten-free beef stock

2 Tbsp. tomato paste

1 Tbsp. instant espresso coffee powder

1 tsp. packed brown sugar

1 tsp. dried thyme

1 tsp. dried rosemary

½ tsp. sea salt

¼ tsp. pepper

1. Spray slow cooker with non-stick cooking spray.

2. In crock, combine onion, carrots, turnip, and celery. Top with beef.

3. Whisk together stock, tomato paste, espresso coffee powder, brown sugar, thyme, rosemary, salt, and pepper. Pour over beef and vegetables in crock.

4. Cover and cook on low for 8–9 hours.

Serving suggestion:

Serve over cooked brown rice or quinoa.

Calories: 240
Fat: 12.5g
Sodium: 370mg
Carbs: 10g
Sugar: 5g
Protein: 23.5g

- Gluten-Free
- Dairy-Free
- Soy-Free
- Nut-Free
- Low-Cal

- Low-Fat
- Low-Sodium
- Low-Carb
- Low-Sugar
- High-Protein

Savory Pork Roast

Mary Louise Martin, Boyd, WI

Makes 4–6 servings
Prep. Time: 15 minutes & Cooking Time: 3½–4½ hours & Ideal slow cooker size: oval 6-qt.

4 lb. boneless pork butt roast
1 tsp. ground ginger
1 Tbsp. fresh minced rosemary
½ tsp. mace or nutmeg
1 tsp. coarsely ground black pepper
2 tsp. salt
2 cups water

1. Grease interior of slow cooker crock.

2. Place roast in slow cooker.

3. In a bowl, mix spices and seasonings together. Sprinkle half on top of roast, pushing down on spices to encourage them to stick.

4. Flip roast and sprinkle with rest of spices, again, pushing down to make them stick.

5. Pour 2 cups water around the edge, being careful not to wash spices off meat.

6. Cover. Cook on Low 3½–4½ hours, or until instant-read meat thermometer registers 140°F when stuck into center of roast.

Calories: 480
Fat: 15g
Sodium: 1100mg
Carbs: .5g
Sugar: 0g
Protein: 81.5g

- Gluten-Free
- Dairy-Free
- Soy-Free
- Nut-Free
- High-Protein
- Low-Carb
- Low-Sugar

Brown Sugar Pork Chops

Andrea Maher, Dunedin, FL

Makes 6 servings

Prep. Time: 5 minutes ❧ *Cooking Time: 6–8 hours* ❧ *Ideal slow cooker size: 5- or 6-qt.*

2 Tbsp. garlic powder

2 tsp. Dijon mustard

3 Tbsp. apple cider vinegar

¼ teaspoon pepper

¼ teaspoon kosher salt

⅓ cup water

¼ cup brown sugar or ¼ cup sugar-free maple syrup

3 cups pineapple slices

24 oz. pork chops

½ cup chopped celery

1. Combine all ingredients in slow cooker.

2. Cover and cook on high for 3–4 hours or on low for 6–8 hours.

Calories: 230
Fat: 4g
Sodium: 180mg
Carbs: 21.5g
Sugar: 16g
Protein: 26.5g

- Low-Carb
- High-Protein
- Gluten-Free
- Dairy-Free
- Nut-Free

- Low-Fat
- Low-Cal
- Low-Sodium
- High-Protein

Raspberry Balsamic Pork Chops

Hope Comerford, Clinton Township, MI

Makes 4–6 servings

Prep. Time: 5 minutes ❧ Cooking Time: 7–8 hours ❧ Ideal slow cooker size: 3-qt.

4–5 lbs. thick-cut pork chops

¼ cup raspberry balsamic vinegar

2 Tbsp. olive oil

½ tsp. kosher salt

½ tsp. garlic powder

¼ tsp. basil

¼ cup water

1. Place pork chops in slow cooker.

2. In a small bowl, mix together the remaining ingredients. Pour over the pork chops.

3. Cover and cook on low for 7–8 hours.

Calories: 475
Fat: 16g
Sodium: 360mg
Carbs: 0g
Sugar: 0g
Protein: 76.5g

- Gluten-Free
- Dairy-Free
- Low-Sodium
- Soy-Free

- Nut-Free
- High-Protein
- Sugar-Free
- Carb-Free

Carnitas

Hope Comerford, Clinton Township, MI

Makes 12 servings
Prep. Time: 10 minutes ♣ Cooking Time: 10–12 hours ♣ Ideal slow cooker size: 4-qt.

2 lb. pork shoulder roast

1½ tsp. kosher salt

½ tsp. pepper

2 tsp. cumin

5 cloves garlic, minced

1 tsp. oregano

3 bay leaves

2 cups gluten-free chicken stock

2 Tbsp. lime juice

1 tsp. lime zest

12 6-inch gluten-free white corn tortillas

1. Place pork shoulder roast in crock.

2. Mix together the salt, pepper, cumin, garlic, and oregano. Rub it onto the pork roast.

3. Place the bay leaves around the pork roast, then pour in the chicken stock around the roast, being careful not to wash off the spices.

4. Cover and cook on low for 10–12 hours.

5. Remove the roast with a slotted spoon, as well as the bay leaves. Shred the pork between 2 forks, then replace the shredded pork in the crock and stir.

6. Add the lime juice and lime zest to the crock and stir.

7. Serve on warmed white corn tortillas.

Calories: 220
Fat: 8g
Sodium: 390mg
Carbs: 14.5g
Sugar: 1g
Protein: 22.5g

- Gluten-Free
- Dairy-Free
- Soy-Free
- Nut-Free
- High-Protein

- Low-Cal
- Low-Fat
- Low-Sodium
- Low-Sugar
- High-Protein

Salsa Verde Pork

Hope Comerford, Clinton Township, MI

Makes 6 servings
Prep. Time: 20 minutes & Cooking Time: 6–6½ hours & Ideal slow cooker size: 4-qt.

1½ lb. boneless pork loin
1 large sweet onion, halved and sliced
2 large tomatoes, chopped
1 16-oz. jar salsa verde (green salsa)
½ cup dry white wine
4 cloves garlic, minced
1 tsp. cumin
½ tsp. chili powder

1. Place the pork loin in the crock and add the rest of the ingredients on top.

2. Cover and cook on low for 6–6½ hours.

3. Break apart the pork with 2 forks and mix with contents of crock.

Serving suggestion:

Serve over cooked brown rice or quinoa.

Calories: 230
Fat: 5.5g
Sodium: 525mg
Carbs: 13g
Sugar: 7g
Protein: 27.45g

- Gluten-Free
- Dairy-Free
- Soy-Free
- Nut-Free

- Low-Cal
- Low-Fat
- Low-Sugar
- High-Protein

Korean Inspired BBQ Shredded Pork

Hope Comerford, Clinton Township, MI

Makes 8–10 servings

Prep. Time: 8–10 minutes ⚹ Cooking Time: 8–10 hours ⚹ Ideal slow cooker size: 3-qt.

1 medium onion

1 McIntosh apple, peeled, cored

5 cloves garlic

¼ cup rice vinegar

1 tsp. gluten-free hot sauce

2 Tbsp. low-sodium gluten-free soy sauce

1 Tbsp. ginger

1 Tbsp. chili powder

¼ tsp. red pepper flakes

3 Tbsp. brown sugar

1 cup ketchup

2–3 lb. pork sirloin tip roast

1. In a food processor, puree the onion, apple, and garlic. Pour this mixture in a bowl and mix it with the rice vinegar, hot sauce, soy sauce, ginger, chili powder, red pepper flakes, brown sugar, and ketchup.

2. Place the pork roast into your crock. Pour the sauce over the top and turn it so it's covered on all sides.

3. Cover and cook on low 8–10 hours.

4. Remove the pork roast and shred it between 2 forks. Return the shredded pork to the crock and mix it through the sauce.

Serving suggestion:

Serve over brown rice or quinoa with a side of bok choi sautéed in toasted sesame seed oil and red pepper flakes.

Calories: 210
Fat: 2.5g
Sodium: 560mg
Carbs: 15.5g
Sugar: 11g
Protein: 30g

- Gluten-Free
- Dairy-Free
- Low-Cal
- Low-Fat
- High-Protein

Frogmore Stew

Janie Steele, Moore, OK

Makes 4–6 servings
Prep. Time: 20–30 minutes ☙ Cooking Time: 6–8 hours ☙ Ideal slow cooker size: 6- or 7-qt.

1 pkg. polish sausage or spicy sausage

crab boil seasoning bag

2½ lbs. small new potatoes

8 ears frozen corn on the cob

1½ Tbsp. Old Bay seasoning

1½ –2 lbs. large raw shrimp, unpeeled

4 quarts water

Optional 5–6 cups fresh salad greens

1. Slice sausage in 1½–2-inch pieces and place in resealable plastic bag.

2. Add crab boil bag (unopened) to bag along with potatoes, corn, and Old Bay seasoning. Mix to coat and place in slow cooker.

3. Add water and cook on low 6–8 hours. Add shrimp during the last 30 minutes of cooking time.

Serving suggestion:

Serve right out of the cooker once liquid is drained or pour on a cookie sheet/newspaper in center of the table. Serve salad on the side if desired.

Calories: 640
Fat: 23g
Sodium: 630mg
Carbs: 65g
Sugar: 8g
Protein: 31g

- Gluten-Free
- Dairy-Free
- Soy-Free
- Nut-Free
- Low-Sugar
- High-Protein

Spiced Cod

Hope Comerford, Clinton Township, MI

Makes 4–6 servings
Prep. Time: 8 minutes   ♣   Cooking Time: 2 hours   ♣   Ideal slow cooker size: 4- or 5-qt.

4–6 cod filets

½ cup thinly sliced red onion

1½ tsp. garlic powder

1½ tsp. onion powder

½ tsp. cumin

¼ tsp. Ancho chili pepper

1 lime, juiced

⅓ cup vegetable broth

1. Place fish in the crock. Place the onions on top.

2. Mix together the remaining ingredients and pour over the fish.

3. Cover and cook on low for 2 hours, or until fish flakes easily with a fork.

Serving suggestion:

Serve on a bed of quinoa or brown rice and with Lemony Garlic Asparagus (page 235).

Calories: 200
Fat: 1.5g
Sodium: 190mg
Carbs: 3.5g
Sugar: 1g
Protein: 41.5g

- Gluten-Free
- Dairy-Free
- High-Protein
- Low-Sodium
- Soy-Free
- Nut-Free

- Low-Cal
- Low-Fat
- Low-Carb
- Low-Sugar
- Paleo

Herbed Flounder

Dorothy VanDeest, Memphis, TX

Makes 6 servings
Prep. Time: 10 minutes ⚘ *Cooking Time: 2–3 hours* ⚘ *Ideal slow cooker size: 6-qt.*

2 lbs. flounder filets, fresh or frozen

¾ cup gluten-free, low-sodium chicken broth or stock

2 Tbsp. lemon juice

2 Tbsp. dried chives

2 Tbsp. dried minced onion

½–1 tsp. leaf marjoram

4 Tbsp. chopped fresh parsley

½ tsp. sea salt

1. Wipe fish as dry as possible. Cut fish into portions to fit slow cooker.

2. Combine broth and lemon juice. Stir in remaining ingredients.

3. Cover and cook on high 2–3 hours, or until fish is flaky.

Calories: 385
Fat: 11g
Sodium: 400mg
Carbs: 2g
Sugar: 1g
Protein: 65g

- Gluten-Free
- Dairy-Free
- Low-Cal
- Low-Fat
- Low-Carb
- Low-Sugar
- High-Protein
- Paleo

Cajun Catfish

Hope Comerford, Clinton Township, MI

Makes 4 servings
Prep. Time: 5 minutes & *Cooking Time: 2 hours* & *Ideal slow cooker size: 6-qt.*

4–6 oz. catfish filets

2 tsp. paprika

I tsp. black pepper

I tsp. oregano

I tsp. dried thyme

½ tsp. garlic powder

½ tsp. kosher salt

½ tsp. parsley flakes

¼ tsp. cayenne pepper

I Tbsp. coconut oil

1. Pat the catfish filets dry.

2. Mix together the paprika, black pepper, oregano, thyme, garlic powder, salt, parsley flakes, and cayenne.

3. Place parchment paper in your crock and push it down so it forms against the inside of the crock. Place the coconut oil in the crock.

4. Coat each side of the catfish filet with the spice mixture, then place them in the crock.

5. Cover and cook on low for about 2 hours, or until the fish flakes easily with a fork.

Calories: 240
Fat: 13.5g
Sodium: 460mg
Carbs: 1.5g
Sugar: 0g
Protein: 26.5g

- Gluten-Free
- Dairy-Free
- Soy-Free
- Nut-Free
- Low-Cal

- Low-Fat
- Sugar-Free
- High-Protein
- Low-Carb
- Paleo

Faked You Out Alfredo

Sue Hamilton, Benson, AZ

Makes 4 servings
Prep. Time: 5 minutes ❀ Cooking Time: 6 hours ❀ Ideal slow cooker size: 3-qt.

1 lb. bag of frozen cauliflower

1 13.5-oz. can light coconut milk

½ cup diced onion

2 cloves garlic, minced

1 Tbsp. vegetable stock concentrate

Salt and pepper to taste

1. Place the frozen cauliflower, coconut milk, onion, garlic, and the vegetable stock concentrate in your crock. Stir mixture to blend in the stock concentrate.

2. Cover and cook on low for 6 hours.

3. Place cooked mixture in blender and process until smooth.

4. Add salt and pepper to taste.

Serving suggestion:

Serve over cooked pasta, cooked sliced potatoes, or any other vegetable.

TIP

My husband loves this on pasta with cooked mushrooms mixed in. This sauce can be made ahead of time and refrigerated.

Calories: 205
Fat: 5g
Sodium: 300mg
Carbs: 36g
Sugar: 7g
Protein: 7g

- Gluten-Free
- Dairy-Free
- Vegan
- Low-Cal

- Vegetarian
- Low-Fat
- Low-Sugar

Spicy Orange Tofu

Sue Hamilton, Benson, AZ

Makes 3 servings
Prep. Time: 5 minutes ⚘ *Cooking Time: 5 hours* ⚘ *Ideal slow cooker size: 3-qt.*

12½ oz. extra firm gluten-free tofu, drained and diced

1½ cups orange marmalade (natural or low-sugar is best)

1 tsp. powdered ginger

1 tsp. minced garlic

1 Tbsp. balsamic vinegar

1 tsp. Sriracha hot chili sauce or to taste

12-oz. bag of mixed stir-fry vegetables

1. Place the drained tofu in the crock.

2. Mix together the marmalade, ginger, garlic, vinegar, and hot chili sauce. Pour over the tofu, but don't mix as it will break up the tofu.

3. Cover and cook on low for 4 hours.

4. Add the stir-fry vegetables on top and cook for one hour longer.

Serving suggestion:

Serve over brown rice.

Calories: 590
Fat: 7.5g
Sodium: 150mg
Carbs: 125.5g
Sugar: 97.5g
Protein: 16g

- Gluten-Free
- Dairy-Free
- Vegan
- Vegetarian
- Low-Sodium
- Low-Fat

Batilgian

Donna Treloar, Muncie, IN

Makes 4–6 servings
Prep. Time: 15–20 minutes ☙ Cooking Time: 3 hours ☙ Ideal slow cooker size: 5- or 6-qt.

1 large Spanish onion, diced

5 Tbsp. olive oil, divided

4 celery ribs, cut in 1-inch pieces

2 cups fresh green beans, trimmed, cut in 2-inch pieces

3 bay leaves

3 garlic cloves, pressed

2 Tbsp. finely chopped fresh basil, or 2 tsp. dry basil

1 large eggplant, cubed

salt and pepper to taste

28-oz. can tomatoes with juice

2 Tbsp. fresh lemon juice

2 Tbsp. capers, optional

1. In a large skillet, sauté onions in 3 Tbsp. olive oil.

2. Add celery. Cover and cook 5 minutes.

3. Add green beans, bay leaves, garlic, basil, and eggplant. Cover and cook 7 minutes.

4. Transfer mixture to slow cooker.

5. Sprinkle with salt and pepper. Drizzle remaining 2 Tbsp. oil over all.

6. Top with tomatoes and juice.

7. Cover and cook on low 3 hours, stirring gently once or twice.

8. Remove bay leaves. Add lemon juice and capers if you wish, just before serving.

Serving suggestion:
Serve alongside your favorite gluten-free crusty bread.

Calories: 210
Fat: 14.5g
Sodium: 220mg
Carbs: 19.5g
Sugar: 11g
Protein: 4g

- Gluten-Free
- Dairy-Free
- Vegan
- Vegetarian
- Low-Sodium
- Low-Cal
- Low-Sugar

Fresh Veggie Lasagna

Deanne Gingrich, Lancaster, PA

Makes 4–6 servings

Prep. Time: 30 minutes ⚬ Cooking Time: 4 hours ⚬ Ideal slow cooker size: 4- or 5-qt.

1½ cups shredded low-fat mozzarella cheese

½ cup low-fat ricotta cheese

⅓ cup grated Parmesan cheese

1 egg, lightly beaten

1 tsp. dried oregano

¼ tsp. garlic powder

3 cups marinara sauce, divided

1 medium zucchini, diced, divided

4 uncooked gluten-free lasagna noodles

4 cups fresh baby spinach, divided

1 cup fresh mushrooms, sliced, divided

1. Grease interior of slow cooker crock.

2. In a bowl, mix together mozzarella, ricotta, and Parmesan cheeses, egg, oregano, and garlic powder. Set aside.

3. Spread ½ cup marinara sauce in crock.

4. Sprinkle with half the zucchini.

5. Spoon ⅓ of cheese mixture over zucchini.

6. Break 2 noodles into large pieces to cover cheese layer.

7. Spread ½ cup marinara over noodles.

8. Top with half the spinach and then half the mushrooms.

9. Repeat layers, ending with cheese mixture, and then sauce. Press layers down firmly.

10. Cover and cook on low for 4 hours, or until vegetables are as tender as you like them and noodles are fully cooked.

11. Let stand 15 minutes so lasagna can firm up before serving.

Calories: 260
Fat: 11g
Sodium: 690mg
Carbs: 25g
Sugar: 6.5g
Protein: 15.5g

- Gluten-Free
- Vegetarian
- Soy-Free
- Nut-Free
- Low-Cal
- Low-Fat
- Low-Sugar

Filled Acorn Squash

Teresa Martin, New Holland, PA

Makes 4 servings
Prep. Time: 20–30 minutes ♣ Cooking Time: 5–10 hours ♣ Ideal slow cooker size: oval 7-qt.

2 medium acorn squash, about 1¼ lbs. each

2 Tbsp. water

15-oz. can black beans, drained, rinsed

½ cup pine nuts, raw, or toasted if you have time

1 large tomato, coarsely chopped

2 green onions, thinly sliced

1 tsp. ground cumin

½ tsp. black pepper, divided

2 tsp. olive oil

½–¾ cup shredded Monterey Jack cheese

1. Grease interior of slow cooker crock.

2. Place washed whole squashes in slow cooker. Spoon in water.

3. Cover and cook on high for 4–6 hours on high or 7–9 hours on low, or until squashes are tender when you pierce them with a fork.

4. While squashes are cooking, mix together beans, pine nuts, tomato, green onions, cumin, and ¼ tsp. black pepper. Set aside.

5. Use sturdy tongs, or wear oven mitts to lift squashes out of cooker. Let cool until you can cut them in half and scoop out the seeds.

6. Brush cut sides and cavity of each squash half with olive oil.

7. Sprinkle all 4 cut sides with remaining black pepper.

8. Spoon heaping ½ cup of bean mixture into each halved squash, pressing down gently to fill cavity.

9. Return halves to slow cooker. Cover and cook on high another hour, or on low another 2 hours, until vegetables are as tender as you like them and thoroughly hot.

10. Uncover and sprinkle with cheese just before serving. When cheese has melted, put a filled half squash on each diner's plate.

Calories: 450
Fat: 20.5g
Sodium: 350mg
Carbs: 56.5g
Sugar: 2g
Protein: 17g

- Gluten-Free
- Vegetarian
- Soy-Free
- Low-Sodium
- Low-Sugar

Main Dishes 221

Vegetable Stuffed Peppers

Shirley Hinh, Wayland, IA

Makes 8 servings
Prep. Time: 20 minutes   •   Cooking Time: 6–8 hours   •   Ideal slow cooker size: 6-qt.

4 large green, red, or yellow bell peppers

½ cup brown rice

¼ cup minced onions

¼ cup black olives, sliced

2 tsp. gluten-free soy sauce or Bragg's liquid aminos

¼ tsp. black pepper

1 clove garlic, minced

28-oz. can low-sodium whole tomatoes

6-oz. can low-sodium tomato paste

15¼-oz. can corn or kidney beans, drained

1. Cut tops off peppers (reserve) and remove seeds. Stand peppers up in slow cooker.

2. Mix remaining ingredients in a bowl. Stuff peppers. (You'll have leftover filling.)

3. Place pepper tops back on peppers. Pour remaining filling over the stuffed peppers and work down in between the peppers.

4. Cover and cook on low 6–8 hours, or until the peppers are done to your liking.

5. If you prefer, you may add ½ cup tomato juice if recipe is too dry.

6. Cut peppers in half and serve.

Serving suggestion:

Drizzle with Greek yogurt.

Calories: 180
Fat: 2g
Sodium: 420mg
Carbs: 34g
Sugar: 11g
Protein: 8g

- Gluten-Free
- Dairy-Free
- Low-Cal
- Vegetarian
- Vegan
- Nut-Free
- Low-Fat

Side Dishes & Vegetables

Stewed Tomatoes

Colleen Heatwole, Burton, MI

Makes 6 servings
Prep. Time: 20 minutes ♣ Cooking Time: 3 hours ♣ Ideal slow cooker size: 6-qt.

½ cup finely chopped onion

½ cup diced green pepper

½ cup celery

1 Tbsp. olive oil

6 cups peeled, coarsely chopped fresh tomatoes (or 2 quarts canned)

1 Tbsp. brown sugar

1 tsp. salt

¾ tsp. dried basil

1. Combine onion, green pepper, and celery with 1 Tbsp. olive oil. Sauté on stovetop until tender. Transfer to slow cooker.

2. Add remaining ingredients.

3. Cover and cook in slow cooker 3 hours on high.

Calories: 70
Fat: 2.5g
Sodium: 400mg
Carbs: 11g
Sugar: 8g
Protein: 2g

- Gluten-Free
- Dairy-Free
- Low-Cal
- Low-Fat
- Vegetarian
- Vegan
- Nut-Free
- Soy-Free
- Low-Carb

Baked Tomatoes

Lizzie Ann Yoder, Hartville, OH

Makes 4 servings

Prep. Time: 10 minutes ❧ *Cooking Time: 45 minutes–1 hour* ❧ *Ideal slow cooker size: 2½- or 3-qt.*

2 tomatoes, each cut in half

½ Tbsp. olive oil

½ tsp. parsley, chopped, or ¼ tsp. dry parsley flakes

¼ tsp. dried oregano

¼ tsp. dried basil

1. Spray slow cooker crock with nonfat cooking spray. Place tomato halves in crock.

2. Drizzle oil over tomatoes. Sprinkle with remaining ingredients.

3. Cover. Cook on high 45 minutes–1 hour.

Calories: 30
Fat: 2g
Sodium: 0mg
Carbs: 3.5g
Sugar: 2.5g
Protein: 1g

- Gluten-Free
- Dairy-Free
- Vegan
- Vegetarian
- Soy-Free
- Nut-Free

- Low-Cal
- Low-Fat
- Sodium-Free
- Low-Carb
- Low-Sugar
- Paleo

Cauliflower Cassoulet

Susie Shenk Wenger, Lancaster, PA

Makes 6 servings
Prep. Time: 30 minutes ❧ Cooking Time: 4–6 hours ❧ Ideal slow cooker size: 6-qt.

I cup uncooked brown rice
½ tsp. kosher salt
2 cups water
I cup sliced fresh mushrooms
I large sweet onion, chopped
½ cup chopped red bell pepper
3 cloves garlic, chopped
I Tbsp. butter
I Tbsp. olive oil
I large head cauliflower, chopped
½ cup diced Parmesan cheese
I tsp. dried basil
½ tsp. dried oregano
salt and pepper, to taste
juice and zest of I lemon

1. Put rice and ½ tsp. salt in lightly greased slow cooker. Pour water over rice.

2. Sprinkle in mushrooms, onion, bell pepper, and garlic. Sprinkle lightly with salt and pepper. Dot with butter and drizzle with olive oil.

3. Sprinkle in cauliflower and diced Parmesan. Sprinkle with basil and oregano, adding salt and pepper to taste.

4. Cover and cook on Low for 4–6 hours, until rice is cooked and cauliflower is tender.

5. Drizzle with lemon juice and zest before serving.

Calories: 250
Fat: 8g
Sodium: 400mg
Carbs: 38.5g
Sugar: 6.5g
Protein: 8.5g

- Gluten-Free
- Soy-Free
- Vegetarian
- Low-Sodium

- Low-Cal
- Nut-Free
- Low-Fat
- Low-Sugar

Slow Cooker Beets

Hope Comerford, Clinton Township, MI

Makes 4–6 servings
Prep. Time: 10 minutes & Cooking Time: 3–4 hours & Ideal slow cooker size: 3-qt.

4–6 large beets, scrubbed well and tops removed

3 Tbsp. olive oil

I tsp. sea salt

¼ tsp. pepper

3 Tbsp. balsamic vinegar

I Tbsp. lemon juice

1. Use foil to make a packet around each beet.

2. Divide the olive oil, salt, pepper, balsamic vinegar, and lemon juice evenly between each packet.

3. Place each beet packet into the slow cooker.

4. Cover and cook on low for 3–4 hours, or until the beets are tender when poked with a knife.

5. Remove each beet packet from the crock and allow to cool and let the steam escape. Once cool enough to handle, use a paring knife to gently peel the skin off each beet. Cut into bite-sized pieces and serve with juice from the packet over the top.

Calories: 140
Fat: 8.5g
Sodium: 570mg
Carbs: 14.5g
Sugar: 10.5g
Protein: 2g

- Gluten-Free
- Dairy-Free
- Vegan
- Vegetarian
- Low-Sugar

- Low-Cal
- Low-Fat
- Soy-Free
- Nut-Free

Lemony Garlic Asparagus

Hope Comerford, Clinton Township, MI

Makes 4 servings

Prep. Time: 5 minutes ❧ *Cooking Time: 1½–2 hours* ❧ *Ideal slow cooker size: 2- or 3-qt.*

I lb. asparagus, bottom inch (tough part) removed

I Tbsp. olive oil

1½ Tbsp. lemon juice

3–4 cloves garlic, peeled and minced

¼ tsp. salt

⅛ tsp. pepper

1. Spray crock with non-stick spray.

2. Lay asparagus at bottom of crock and coat with the olive oil.

3. Pour the lemon juice over the top, then sprinkle with the garlic, salt, and pepper.

4. Cover and cook on low for 1½–2 hours.

Serving suggestion:

Garnish with diced pimento, garlic, and lemon zest.

Calories: 60
Fat: 3.5g
Sodium: 150mg
Carbs: 5.5g
Sugar: 2.5g
Protein: 2.5g

- Gluten-Free
- Dairy-Free
- Vegan
- Vegetarian
- Low-Sugar
- Low-Cal
- Low-Fat
- Low-Sodium
- Soy-Free
- Nut-Free
- Low-Carb

Mediterranean Onions

Barbara Warren, Folsom, PA

Makes 4–6 servings
Prep. Time: 25 minutes ⚬ Cooking Time: 4–8 hours ⚬ Ideal slow cooker size: 3-qt.

4 large yellow onions, sliced in thin rings

½ tsp. freshly ground pepper

I tsp. salt

¼ tsp. turmeric

I tsp. dried thyme

½ tsp. dried basil

I Tbsp. butter

I Tbsp. olive oil

I Tbsp. fresh lemon juice

⅓ cup chopped fresh parsley

⅓ cup crumbled feta cheese

oil-cured black olives, pitted, chopped, optional

1. Combine onions, pepper, salt, turmeric, thyme, basil, butter, and olive oil in slow cooker.

2. Cover and cook on low for 4–8 hours, stirring once or twice, until onions are soft and getting brown.

3. Remove onions to serving dish. Gently stir in lemon juice and parsley. Sprinkle with feta and optional black olives. Serve hot or room temperature.

TIP

Add more lemon juice or even some lemon zest if the onions need some brightening up.

Calories: 120
Fat: 7.5g
Sodium: 560mg
Carbs: 12.5g
Sugar: 5.5g
Protein: 3g

- Gluten-Free
- Vegetarian
- Low-Cal
- Low-Sugar
- Soy-Free
- Nut-Free
- Low-Fat

Broccoli and Bell Peppers

Frieda Weisz, Aberdeen, SD

Makes 8 servings

Prep. Time: 20 minutes ♣ Cooking Time: 4–5 hours ♣ Ideal slow cooker size: 3½- or 4-qt.

2 lbs. fresh broccoli, trimmed and chopped into bite-size pieces

1 clove garlic, minced

1 green or red bell pepper, cut into thin slices

1 onion, peeled and cut into slices

4 Tbsp. low-sodium gluten-free soy sauce or Bragg's liquid aminos

½ tsp. salt

dash of black pepper

1 Tbsp. sesame seeds, optional, as garnish

1. Combine all ingredients except sesame seeds in slow cooker.

2. Cook on low for 4–5 hours. Top with sesame seeds.

Serving suggestion:

Serve over cooked brown rice.

Calories: 60
Fat: .5g
Sodium: 690mg
Carbs: 10.5g
Sugar: 3.5g
Protein: 4.5g

- Gluten-Free
- Dairy-Free
- Vegetarian
- Low-Cal
- Nut-Free
- Low-Fat
- Low-Sugar
- Low-Carb
- Paleo

Orange-Glazed Carrots

Cyndie Marrara, Port Matilda, PA

Makes 6 servings
Prep. Time: 5–10 minutes ❧ Cooking Time: 3–4 hours ❧ Ideal slow cooker size: 3½-qt.

32-oz. (2 lbs.) pkg. baby carrots

⅓ cup turbinado sugar

2–3 oranges, squeezed for juice to make approx. ½ cup juice

3 Tbsp. coconut oil, melted

¾ tsp. cinnamon

¼ tsp. nutmeg

2 Tbsp. cornstarch

¼ cup water

1. Combine all ingredients except cornstarch and water in slow cooker.

2. Cover. Cook on low 3–4 hours, until carrots are tender crisp.

3. Put carrots in serving dish and keep warm, reserving cooking juices. Put reserved juices in small saucepan. Bring to boil.

4. Mix cornstarch and water in small bowl until blended. Add to juices. Boil one minute or until thickened, stirring constantly.

5. Pour over carrots and serve.

Serving suggestion:
Sprinkle with orange zest before serving.

Calories: 170
Fat: 7g
Sodium: 120mg
Carbs: 27.5g
Sugar: 19g
Protein: 1g

- Gluten-Free
- Dairy-Free
- Soy-Free
- Nut-Free

- Low-Sodium
- Low-Cal
- Low-Fat

Wild Mushrooms Italian

Connie Johnson, Loudon, NH

Makes 4–5 servings

Prep. Time: 20 minutes ⚹ Cooking Time: 6–8 hours ⚹ Ideal slow cooker size: 5-qt.

2 large onions, chopped

3 large red bell peppers, chopped

3 large green bell peppers, chopped

2–3 Tbsp. olive oil

12-oz. pkg. oyster mushrooms, cleaned and chopped

4 garlic cloves, minced

3 fresh bay leaves

10 fresh basil leaves, chopped

1 tsp. salt

1½ tsp. pepper

28-oz. can Italian plum tomatoes, crushed, or chopped

1. Sauté onions and peppers in oil in skillet until soft. Stir in mushrooms and garlic. Sauté just until mushrooms begin to turn brown. Pour into slow cooker.

2. Add remaining ingredients. Stir well.

3. Cover. Cook on low 6–8 hours. Remove bay leaves and serve.

Calories: 210
Fat: 8g
Sodium: 780mg
Carbs: 33g
Sugar: 17g
Protein: 8g

- Gluten-Free
- Dairy-Free
- Soy-Free
- Vegetarian

- Vegan
- Low-Cal
- Low-Fat
- Nut-Free

Brussels Sprouts with Pimentos

Donna Lantgon, Rapid City, SD

Makes 8 servings
Prep. Time: 10 minutes ⚜ *Cooking Time: 6 hours* ⚜ *Ideal slow cooker size: 3½- or 4-qt.*

2 lbs. Brussels sprouts

¼ tsp. dried oregano

½ tsp. dried basil

2-oz. jar pimentos, drained

¼ cup, or 1 small can sliced black olives, drained

1 Tbsp. olive oil

½ cup water

1. Combine all ingredients in slow cooker.

2. Cook on low 6 hours, or until sprouts are just tender.

Calories: 70	• Gluten-Free	• Low-Fat
Fat: 2.5g	• Dairy-Free	• Low-Cal
Sodium: 60mg	• Vegan	• Low-Sodium
Carbs: 11g	• Vegetarian	• Low-Carb
Sugar: 2.5g	• Soy-Free	• Low-Sugar
Protein: 4g	• Nut-Free	• Paleo

Armenian Eggplant

Donna Treloar, Muncie, IN

Makes 6 servings
Prep. Time: 30 minutes   ♣   Cooking Time: 3–4 hours   ♣   Ideal slow cooker size: 6-qt.

1 large sweet onion, diced

4 garlic cloves, peeled and chopped

4 ribs celery, diced

2 cups fresh green beans, cut in 2-inch pieces

3 Tbsp. olive oil

2 tsp. dried basil

¼ tsp. black pepper

1 tsp. salt

1 medium eggplant, cubed

28-oz. can tomatoes with juice

2 Tbsp. lemon juice

2 Tbsp. capers

1. In slow cooker, combine onion, garlic, celery, green beans, olive oil, basil, black pepper, and salt.

2. Layer in eggplant. Pour tomatoes and juice over all.

3. Cover and cook on low 3–4 hours, until vegetables are tender.

4. Add lemon juice and capers. Stir gently. Serve hot or room temperature with good bread and olive oil for dipping.

Calories: 140
Fat: 7.5g
Sodium: 640mg
Carbs: 18.5g
Sugar: 11g
Protein: 3.5g

- Gluten-Free
- Dairy-Free
- Vegan
- Vegetarian

- Low-Cal
- Nut-Free
- Low-Fat

Eggplant Italian

Melanie Thrower, McPherson, KS

Makes 6–8 servings

Prep. Time: 30 minutes ❧ *Cooking Time: 4 hours* ❧ *Ideal slow cooker size: 4- or 5-qt. oval*

2 eggplants
¼ cup Egg Beaters
24 oz. fat-free cottage cheese
¼ tsp. salt
black pepper to taste
14-oz. can tomato sauce
2–4 Tbsp. Italian seasoning, according to your taste preference

1. Peel eggplants and cut in ½-inch thick slices. Soak in saltwater for about 5 minutes to remove bitterness. Drain well.

2. Spray slow cooker with fat-free cooking spray.

3. Mix Egg Beaters, cottage cheese, salt, and pepper together in bowl.

4. Mix tomato sauce and Italian seasoning together in another bowl.

5. Spoon a thin layer of tomato sauce into bottom of slow cooker. Top with about one-third of eggplant slices, and then one-third of egg/cheese mixture, and finally one-third of remaining tomato sauce mixture.

6. Repeat those layers twice, ending with seasoned tomato sauce.

7. Cover. Cook on high 4 hours. Allow to rest 15 minutes before serving.

Calories: 130
Fat: 1g
Sodium: 470mg
Carbs: 20g
Sugar: 9.5g
Protein: 13.5g

- Gluten-Free
- Vegetarian
- Soy-Free
- Low-Cal
- Low-Fat
- Nut-Free

Side Dishes & Vegetables ❧ 249

Spicy Roasted Butternut Squash

Marilyn Mowry, Irving, TX

Makes 15–20 servings

Prep. Time: 1 hour ⚜ *Cooking Time: 4–6 hours* ⚜ *Ideal slow cooker size: 6-qt.*

¼ cup olive oil

2 tsp. ground cinnamon, divided

½ tsp. ground cumin

1¾ tsp. salt, divided

5 lb. butternut squash, split in quarters and seeds removed

2 carrots, diced

1 large white onion, diced

2 Granny Smith apples, peeled, cored, and quartered

4 chipotles in adobo sauce, seeds scraped out, chopped

roughly 10 cups gluten-free chicken stock

1. Mix olive oil, 1 tsp. cinnamon, ground cumin, and ¾ tsp. salt in mixing bowl. Brush over the flesh of the quartered squash.

2. Place squash cut side down on a rimmed baking sheet lined with foil.

3. Add carrots, onions, and apples to bowl with oil and toss. Spread on another foil-lined sheet.

4. Roast both trays 40–50 minutes at 425°F until squash is soft and onion mix is golden brown. Scoop out the squash.

5. Put squash, veggie mix, chipotles, 1 tsp. salt, and 1 tsp. cinnamon in slow cooker. Add chicken broth.

6. Cover and cook on high 4 hours or low for 6 hours. Mash with a potato masher or puree with immersion blender.

Calories: 120
Fat: 3g
Sodium: 310mg
Carbs: 21g
Sugar: 6g
Protein: 4g

- Gluten-Free
- Dairy-Free
- Soy-Free
- Low-Cal
- Nut-Free
- Low-Fat
- Low-Sugar

Corn on the Cob

Donna Conto, Saylorsburg, PA

Makes 3–4 servings
Prep. Time: 10 minutes ❧ Cooking Time: 2–3 hours ❧ Ideal slow cooker size: 5- or 6-qt.

6–8 ears of corn (in husk)
½ cup water

1. Remove silk from corn, as much as possible, but leave husks on.

2. Cut off ends of corn so ears can stand in the cooker.

3. Add water.

4. Cover. Cook on low 2–3 hours.

Calories: 160
Fat: 2g
Sodium: 30mg
Carbs: 34g
Sugar: 6g
Protein: 6g

- Gluten-Free
- Dairy-Free
- Vegan
- Vegetarian
- Soy-Free

- Low-Sodium
- Low-Fat
- Low-Cal
- Nut-Free
- Low-Sugar

Garden Chips

MarJanita Geigley, Lancaster, PA

Makes 4 servings

Prep. Time: 15 minutes ⚘ *Cooking Time: 2 hours* ⚘ *Ideal slow cooker size: 3- or 4-qt.*

½ cup gluten-free rolled oats, ground into flour

⅛ tsp. pepper

2 Tbsp. grated Parmesan cheese

3 egg whites

3–4 medium zucchini, cut into ¼-inch slices

1. In small bowl mix together oat flour, pepper, and Parmesan cheese.

2. Place egg whites in another dish and whisk.

3. Dip zucchini in egg whites then into oat flour mixture.

4. Place zucchini into greased slow cooker and cook on low for 1 hour.

5. Turn chips and cook for another hour.

Calories: 120
Fat: 2.5g
Sodium: 100mg
Carbs: 18g
Sugar: 4g
Protein: 8.5g

- Gluten-Free
- Soy-Free
- Vegetarian
- Low-Cal

- Low-Fat
- Low-Sodium
- Low-Sugar
- Nut-Free

Quinoa with Vegetables

Hope Comerford, Clinton Township, MI

Makes 4–6 servings
Prep. Time: 10 minutes ⚬ *Cooking Time: 4–6 hours* ⚬ *Ideal slow cooker size: 3-qt.*

2 cups quinoa

4 cups vegetable stock

½ cup chopped onion

1 Tbsp. olive oil

1 medium red pepper, chopped

1 medium yellow pepper, chopped

1 medium carrot, chopped

3 garlic cloves, minced

½ tsp. sea salt

¼ tsp. pepper

1 Tbsp. fresh cilantro, chopped

1. Place quinoa, vegetable stock, onion, olive oil, red pepper, yellow pepper, carrot, garlic, salt, and pepper into crock and stir.

2. Cook on low for 4–6 hours or until liquid is absorbed and quinoa is tender.

3. Top with fresh cilantro to serve.

Calories: 315
Fat: 7g
Sodium: 690mg
Carbs: 53g
Sugar: 4g
Protein: 10.5g

- Gluten-Free
- Dairy-Free
- Vegan
- Vegetarian

- Low-Sugar
- Low-Cal
- Low-Fat

Cabbage and Potatoes

Deb Kepiro, Strasburg, PA

Makes 4 servings
Prep. Time: 15 minutes   ❧   Cooking Time: 3–6 hours   ❧   Ideal slow cooker size: 4-qt.

I small head green cabbage, sliced thinly

14 small red-skinned potatoes, cut in 1-inch chunks

I small onion, diced

3 Tbsp. olive oil

2 Tbsp. balsamic vinegar

I tsp. kosher salt

½ tsp. black pepper

1. Put all ingredients in slow cooker. Mix well.

2. Cover and cook on high for 3 hours, until potatoes are as tender as you like them.

Calories: 570
Fat: 11g
Sodium: 720mg
Carbs: 108g
Sugar: 15.5g
Protein: 14g

- Gluten-Free
- Dairy-Free
- Soy-Free
- Vegan

- Vegetarian
- Nut-Free
- Low-Fat

"Baked" Sweet Potatoes

Hope Comerford, Clinton Township, MI

Makes 5 potatoes

Prep. Time: 2 minutes 🌿 Cooking Time: 4–5 hours 🌿 Ideal slow cooker size: 5- or 6-qt.

5 sweet potatoes, pierced in several places with a fork or knife

1. Place sweet potatoes in slow cooker.

2. Cover and cook on low for 4–5 hours, or until they are tender when poked with a fork or knife.

Calories: 110
Fat: 0g
Sodium: 70mg
Carbs: 26g
Sugar: 5.5g
Protein: 2g

- Gluten-Free
- Dairy-Free
- Vegetarian
- Vegan
- Soy-Free
- Nut-Free

- Low-Cal
- Low-Fat
- Low-Sodium
- Low-Sugar
- Fat-Free

Autumn Sweet Potatoes

Melinda Wenger, Middleburg, PA

Makes 4 servings
Prep. Time: 20 minutes & Cooking Time: 2–3 hours & Ideal slow cooker size: 4-qt.

4 medium sweet potatoes, peeled, sliced thinly

1 large Granny Smith apple, peeled and diced

zest and juice of ½ orange

½ cup raisins

2 Tbsp. maple syrup

toasted, chopped walnuts, for serving, optional

1. Place sweet potatoes in lightly greased slow cooker.

2. Top with apples, raisins, and orange zest. Drizzle with maple syrup and orange juice.

3. Cover and cook on high for 2–3 hours or until sweet potatoes are tender. Serve sprinkled with walnuts if you wish.

Calories: 230
Fat: 0g
Sodium: 75mg
Carbs: 56.5g
Sugar: 29g
Protein: 3g

- Gluten-Free
- Dairy-Free
- Vegan
- Vegetarian

- Soy-Free
- Low-Cal
- Fat-Free
- Low-Sodium

Thyme Roasted Sweet Potatoes

Hope Comerford, Clinton Township, MI

Makes 6 servings
Prep. Time: 20 minutes ⚬ Cooking Time: 2–3 hours ⚬ Ideal slow cooker size: 4-qt.

4–6 medium sweet potatoes, peeled, cubed

3 Tbsp. olive oil

5–6 large garlic cloves, minced

⅓ cup fresh thyme leaves

½ tsp. kosher salt

¼ tsp. red pepper flakes

1. Place all ingredients into the crock and stir.

2. Cover and cook on low for 7 hours, or until potatoes are tender.

Calories: 160
Fat: 7g
Sodium: 250mg
Carbs: 23.5g
Sugar: 4.5g
Protein: 2g

- Gluten-Free
- Soy-Free
- Dairy-Free
- Nut-Free
- Low-Cal

- Low-Fat
- Vegan
- Vegetarian
- Low-Sodium
- Low-Sugar

Honey Roasted Parsnips, Sweet Potatoes, and Apples

Gloria Yurkiewicz, Washington Boro, PA

Makes 4 servings
Prep. Time: 20 minutes ⚜ *Cooking Time: 5 hours* ⚜ *Ideal slow cooker size: 3-qt.*

1½ cups parsnips, peeled and cubed

1 large sweet potato, peeled and cubed

2 firm red apples, cored and sliced thick

1 Tbsp. coconut oil

1 Tbsp. honey

2 Tbsp. gluten-free soy sauce or Bragg's liquid aminos

¼ tsp. ground ginger

1. Mix parsnips, sweet potatoes, and apples in greased crock. Add remaining ingredients and stir.

2. Cover and cook on low for 5 hours, or until parsnips and potatoes are tender when poked with a fork.

Calories: 160
Fat: 4g
Sodium: 530mg
Carbs: 33g
Sugar: 17.5g
Protein: 2.5g

- Gluten-Free
- Dairy-Free
- Vegetarian
- Low-Cal
- Low-Fat

Quick and Light Sweet Potato Wedges

MarJanita Geigley, Lancaster, PA

Makes 4 servings
Prep. Time: 15 minutes   ♣   Cooking Time: 3–5 hours   ♣   Ideal slow cooker size: 3-qt.

4 sweet potatoes, cut into wedges
2 Tbsp. olive oil
2 tsp. Italian seasoning
3 Tbsp. light gluten-free Italian dressing
1 Tbsp. minced garlic

1. Combine all ingredients in sealable plastic bag and shake well.

2. Pour into slow cooker and cook on low for 3–5 hours.

Serving suggestion:

To make a dipping sauce, mix together Greek yogurt, Sriracha sauce, and minced garlic to taste.

Calories: 180
Fat: 7g
Sodium: 190mg
Carbs: 28.5g
Sugar: 6.5g
Protein: 2.5g

- Gluten-Free
- Dairy-Free
- Vegan
- Vegetarian
- Low-Cal

- Low-Sodium
- Low-Fat
- Nut-Free
- Soy-Free
- Low-Sugar

Crockpot Beans & Rice

Kris Zimmerman, Lititz, PA

Makes 6–8 servings

Prep. Time: 15 minutes ⚬ Cooking Time: 3–4 hours ⚬ Ideal slow cooker size: 3-qt.

3 cups cooked beans of your choice,
rinsed and drained

1 cup brown rice

14.5-oz. can diced tomatoes

1 Tbsp. coconut oil, melted

salt to taste

1 tsp. cumin

½ tsp. garlic powder

2 cups water

diced green chilies, optional

hot sauce or cayenne pepper, optional

1. Place all ingredients in slow cooker and stir well.

2. Cover and cook on high for 2–3 hours. Begin checking at 3–3½ hours to see if your rice is done.

Calories: 240
Fat: 3.5g
Sodium: 110mg
Carbs: 44.5g
Sugar: 3g
Protein: 9.5g

- Gluten-Free
- Dairy-Free
- Soy-Free
- Vegetarian
- Vegan

- Low-Sodium
- Low-Fat
- Low-Cal
- Low-Sugar

Aunt Twila's Beans

Mary Louise Martin, Boyd, WI

Makes 10–12 servings
Prep. Time: 15 minutes ❧ *Cooking Time: 10 hours* ❧ *Ideal slow cooker size: 5-qt.*

5 cups dry pinto beans
2 tsp. ground cumin
1 medium yellow onion, minced
4 minced garlic cloves
9 cups water
3 tsp. salt
3 Tbsp. lemon juice

1. Combine beans, cumin, onion, garlic, and water in slow cooker.

2. Cook on low for 8 hours.

3. Add salt and lemon juice. Stir. Cook on low for another 2 hours.

Calories: 310
Fat: 1g
Sodium: 650mg
Carbs: 56.5g
Sugar: 2.5g
Protein: 19g

- Gluten-Free
- Dairy-Free
- Vegan
- Vegetarian
- Soy-Free

- High-Protein
- Low-Cal
- Low-Fat
- Low-Sugar

Savory Rice

Jane Geigley, Lancaster, PA

Makes 6–8 servings
Prep. Time: 10 minutes ⚬ *Cooking Time: 3–4 hours* ⚬ *Ideal slow cooker size: 4-qt.*

2 cups uncooked short-grain brown rice

5 cups water

1 Tbsp. coconut oil

½ tsp. ground thyme

2 Tbsp. dried parsley

2 tsp. garlic powder

1 tsp. dried basil

1 tsp. salt

1. Mix rice, water, coconut oil, thyme, parsley, garlic powder, basil, and salt.

2. Pour into slow cooker. Cover.

3. Cook on high for 3–4 hours or until water is absorbed.

Calories: 230
Fat: 2.5g
Sodium: 340mg
Carbs: 46g
Sugar: 0g
Protein: 4g

- Gluten-Free
- Dairy-Free
- Soy-Free
- Vegetarian
- Vegan

- Low-Sodium
- Low-Fat
- Low-Cal
- Sugar-Free

Desserts

Fruit Compote Dessert

Beatrice Orgish, Richardson, TX

Makes 8 servings

Prep. Time: 25 minutes ⚜ *Cooking Time: 3–4 hours* ⚜ *Ideal slow cooker size: 4-qt.*

2 medium tart apples, peeled

2 medium fresh peaches, peeled and cubed

2 cups fresh pineapple chunks

1¼ cups fresh pineapple juice

2 Tbsp. honey

2 ¼-inch thick lemon slices

3½-inch cinnamon stick

1 medium firm banana, thinly sliced

whipped cream, optional

sliced almonds, optional

maraschino cherries, optional

1. Cut apples into ¼-inch slices and then in half horizontally. Place in slow cooker.

2. Add peaches, pineapple, pineapple juice, honey, lemon slices, and cinnamon sticks. Cover and cook on low 3–4 hours.

3. Stir in banana slices just before serving. Garnish with whipped cream, sliced almonds, and cherries, if you wish.

Calories: 110
Fat: .5g
Sodium: 0mg
Carbs: 28g
Sugar: 22g
Protein: 1g

- Gluten-Free
- Soy-Free
- Vegetarian

- Low-Fat
- Sodium-Free
- Low-Cal

Drunken Fruit

Dena Mell-Dorchy, Royal Oak, MI

Makes 14 servings

Prep. Time: 25 minutes   ⚙   Cooking Time: 3½–4 hours   ⚙   Ideal slow cooker size: 3- or 4-qt.

¼ cup honey

¼ cup melted coconut oil

½ cup coconut rum

2 Tbsp. quick cooking tapioca, crushed

¼ tsp. salt

2½ cups fresh pineapple chunks

3 firm ripe plums, pitted and cut into wedges

2 medium Granny Smith apples, cored and cut into 1-inch pieces

2 medium pears, cored and cut into 1-inch pieces

2 medium peaches, pitted and cut into wedges

1. In a small bowl combine honey, coconut oil, coconut rum, tapioca, and salt.

2. Combine all fruit in the slow cooker

3. Pour rum mixture over fruit; stir to combine.

4. Cover and cook on low for 3½–4 hours.

Calories: 130
Fat: 4.5g
Sodium: 50mg
Carbs: 22g
Sugar: 17g
Protein: 1g

- Gluten-Free
- Dairy-Free
- Vegetarian
- Low-Fat

- Low-Sodium
- Soy-Free
- Low-Cal

Tropical Fruit

Hope Comerford, Clinton Township, MI

Makes 14 servings
Prep. Time: 15 minutes   Cooking Time: 3½–4 hours   Ideal slow cooker size: 3- or 4-qt.

24 oz. frozen mango, thawed, drained, and cut into 1-inch pieces

20-oz. can pineapple chunks, drained

16 oz. frozen peach slices, unsweetened

12-oz. pkg. soft coconut macaroon cookies, crumbled

½ cup dried cherries

¼ cup maple syrup

¼ cup melted coconut oil

1 tsp. lemon zest

2 Tbsp. lemon juice

1. Spray crock with non-stick spray.

2. Combine mangos, pineapple, peaches, crumbled macaroons, and cherries in crock.

3. In a bowl, mix together the maple syrup, coconut oil, lemon zest, and lemon juice; pour over mixture in slow cooker.

4. Cover and cook on low for 2½–4 hours.

Calories: 240
Fat: 10g
Sodium: 60mg
Carbs: 39g
Sugar: 31.5g
Protein: 1.5g

- Gluten-Free
- Vegetarian
- Low-Sodium

- Soy-Free
- Low-Cal
- Low-Fat

Baked Apples with Dates

Mary E. Wheatley, Mashpee, MA

Makes 8 servings

Prep. Time: 20–25 minutes   ♣   Cooking Time: 2–6 hours   ♣   Ideal slow cooker size: 6-qt. oval, or large enough cooker that the apples can each sit on the floor of the cooker, rather than being stacked

8 medium-sized baking apples

Filling:
¾ cup coarsely chopped dates
3 Tbsp. chopped pecans
¼ cup honey

Topping:
I tsp. ground cinnamon
½ tsp. ground nutmeg
I Tbsp. coconut oil, melted
½ cup water

1. Wash, core, and peel top third of apples.

2. Mix dates and chopped nuts with honey. Stuff into centers of apples where cores had been.

3. Set apples upright in slow cooker.

4. Sprinkle with cinnamon and nutmeg. Pour melted coconut oil evenly over each apple.

5. Add water around inside edge of cooker.

6. Cover. Cook on low 4–6 hours or on high 2–3 hours, or until apples are as tender as you like them.

Calories: 70
Fat: 3.5g
Sodium: 0mg
Carbs: 11g
Sugar: 10.5g
Protein: .5g

- Gluten-Free
- Dairy-Free
- Soy-Free
- Low-Cal
- Low-Fat
- Sodium-Free
- Low-Carb
- Low-Sugar
- Paleo

Festive Applesauce

Dawn Day, Westminster, CA

Makes 12 servings
Prep. Time: 25 minutes ⚘ Cooking Time: 6 hours ⚘ Ideal slow cooker size: 5-qt.

8 medium apples, mixed varieties, peeled and cubed

5 pears, peeled and cubed

1 cup fresh or frozen cranberries

1-inch piece fresh ginger root, minced

3 Tbsp. maple syrup

½ cup apple cider

3 tsp. ground cinnamon

¼ tsp. ground nutmeg

¼ tsp. ground cloves

pinch salt

juice and zest of 1 lemon

1. Combine all ingredients in slow cooker except for lemon zest and juice.

2. Cover and cook on low for 6 hours, until apples and pears are soft and falling apart.

3. Stir in lemon zest and juice. Serve hot, warm, or chilled.

Calories: 130
Fat: .5g
Sodium: 20mg
Carbs: 34.5g
Sugar: 24.5g
Protein: .5g

- Gluten-Free
- Dairy-Free
- Vegan
- Vegetarian
- Nut-Free

- Soy-Free
- Low-Cal
- Low-Fat
- Low-Sodium

Chunky Applesauce

Hope Comerford, Clinton Township, MI

Makes 10 servings
Prep. Time: 20 minutes ☘ Cooking Time: 6–8 hours ☘ Ideal slow cooker size: 3- or 4-qt.

3 lbs. tart apples, peeled, cored, sliced
⅓ cup honey
½ cup water
1 tsp. lemon zest
3 Tbsp. lemon juice
3 cinnamon sticks

1. Spray the crock with non-stick spray.

2. Place all ingredients into the slow cooker. Stir to coat all apples.

3. Cover and cook on low for 6–8 hours.

4. Remove cinnamon sticks and mash applesauce mixture lightly with a potato masher.

Calories: 100
Fat: 0g
Sodium: 0mg
Carbs: 28.5g
Sugar: 23.5g
Protein: .5g

- Gluten-Free
- Dairy-Free
- Vegetarian
- Low-Cal
- Fat-Free
- Sodium-Free
- Soy-Free
- Nut-Free

Pears in Ginger Sauce

Sharon Timpe, Jackson, WI

Makes 6 servings
Prep. Time: 20 minutes   ❧   Cooking Time: 3–5 hours   ❧   Standing Time: 45 minutes   ❧
Ideal slow cooker size: 6-qt.

6 fresh pears with stems
1 cup white wine
⅓ cup honey
½ cup water
3 Tbsp. lemon juice
1 tsp. ground ginger
pinch nutmeg
pinch salt
¼ cup toasted coconut, for serving

1. Peel pears, leaving whole with stems intact.

2. Place pears in greased slow cooker, upright, shaving bottoms slightly if necessary.

3. Combine wine, honey, water, lemon juice, ginger, nutmeg, and salt. Pour evenly over pears.

4. Cover and cook on low for 3–5 hours, or until pears are tender.

5. Allow pears and liquid to cool.

6. To serve, set a pear in a dessert dish, drizzle with sauce, and sprinkle with toasted coconut.

Calories: 220
Fat: 5g
Sodium: 40mg
Carbs: 48g
Sugar: 33.5g
Protein: 1.44g

- Gluten-Free
- Dairy-Free
- Vegetarian
- Low-Sodium
- Soy-Free
- Low-Fat
- Low-Cal

Dates in Cardamom Coffee Syrup

Margaret W. High, Lancaster, PA

Makes 12 servings
Prep. Time: 15 minutes ⚜ Cooking Time: 7–8 hours ⚜ Ideal slow cooker size: 3-qt.

2 cups pitted, whole dried dates

2½ cups very strong, hot coffee

2 Tbsp. turbinado sugar

15 whole green cardamom pods

4-inch cinnamon stick

plain Greek yogurt, for serving

1. Combine dates, coffee, sugar, cardamom, and cinnamon stick in slow cooker.

2. Cover and cook on high for 1 hour. Remove lid and continue to cook on high for 6–7 hours until sauce has reduced.

3. Pour dates and sauce into container and chill in fridge.

4. To serve, put a scoop of Greek yogurt in a small dish and add a few dates on top. Drizzle with a little sauce.

Calories: 80
Fat: 0g
Sodium: 0mg
Carbs: 20.5g
Sugar: 17.5g
Protein: .5g

- Gluten-Free
- Soy-Free
- Vegetarian
- Low-Cal
- Nut-Free
- Fat-Free
- No-Sodium

Quick Yummy Peaches

Willard E. Roth, Elkhart, IN

Makes 6 servings
Prep. Time: 5–20 minutes   Cooking Time: 5 hours   Ideal slow cooker size: 3-qt.

⅓ cup low-fat gluten-free baking mix

⅔ cup gluten-free oats

⅓ cup maple syrup

1 tsp. ground cinnamon

4 cups sliced fresh peaches

½ cup water

1. Mix together baking mix, oats, maple syrup, and cinnamon in greased slow cooker.

2. Stir in peaches and water.

3. Cook on low for at least 5 hours. (If you like a drier cobbler, remove lid for last 15–30 minutes of cooking.)

Calories: 140
Fat: 1g
Sodium: 60mg
Carbs: 33g
Sugar: 20g
Protein: 2g

- Gluten-Free
- Vegetarian
- Dairy-Free
- Nut-Free

- Soy-Free
- Low-Cal
- Low-Fat
- Low-Sodium

Healthy Coconut Apple Crisp

Hope Comerford, Clinton Township, MI

Makes 8–9 servings
Prep. Time: 20 minutes & Cooking Time: 2 hours & Ideal slow cooker size: 3- or 4-qt.

5 medium Granny Smith apples, peeled, cored, sliced

1 Tbsp. cinnamon

¼ tsp. nutmeg

1 tsp. vanilla

Crumble:

1 cup gluten-free oats

½ cup coconut flour

½ cup unsweetened coconut flakes

1 tsp. cinnamon

⅛ tsp. nutmeg

½ tsp. sea salt

2 Tbsp. honey

2 Tbsp. coconut oil, melted

2–3 Tbsp. unsweetened coconut milk

1. Spray crock with non-stick spray

2. In the crock, combine apple slices, cinnamon, nutmeg, and vanilla.

3. In a medium bowl, combine all of the crumble ingredients. If too dry, add a bit more honey or coconut milk. Pour over top of apple mixture.

4. Cover slow cooker and cook on low for 2 hours.

Serving suggestion:

Serve with a scoop of coconut ice cream.

Calories: 240
Fat: 8.5g
Sodium: 230mg
Carbs: 38.5g
Sugar: 18.5g
Protein: 5g

- Gluten-Free
- Dairy-Free
- Vegetarian
- Soy-Free

- Low-Cal
- Low-Fat
- Low-Sodium

Strawberry Mint Crisp

Hope Comerford, Clinton Township, MI

Makes 4 servings
Prep. Time: 20 minutes ⚘ *Cooking Time: 2 hours* ⚘ *Ideal slow cooker size: 2- or 3-qt.*

2½–3 cups sliced strawberries
1 tsp. cinnamon
½ tsp. mint extract
1 tsp. vanilla
3 Tbsp. fresh chopped mint

Crumble:
½ cup gluten-free oats
¼ cup gluten-free oat flour
½ tsp. cinnamon
¼ tsp. salt
1 Tbsp. honey
1 Tbsp. coconut oil, melted
1–2 Tbsp. unsweetened almond or coconut milk

1. Spray crock with non-stick spray.

2. In the crock, combine strawberries, cinnamon, mint extract, vanilla extract, and fresh chopped mint.

3. In a bowl, combine all the crumble ingredients. If it's too dry, add a bit more honey or milk of your choice. Pour this mixture into the crock.

4. Cover and cook on low for 2 hours.

Serving suggestion:
Serve with vanilla Greek yogurt.

Calories: 200
Fat: 6.5g
Sodium: 150mg
Carbs: 31.5g
Sugar: 10.5g
Protein: 5g

- Gluten-Free
- Dairy-Free
- Vegetarian
- Soy-Free
- Nut-Free

- Low-Fat
- Low-Cal
- Low-Sodium
- Low-Sugar

Nectarine Almond Crisp

Hope Comerford, Clinton Township, MI

Makes 8–9 servings
Prep. Time: 10 minutes ⚘ *Cooking Time: 2 hours* ⚘ *Ideal slow cooker size: 3- or 4-qt.*

5 nectarines, cored and sliced
¼ cup slivered almonds
1 tsp. cinnamon
¼ tsp. nutmeg
¼ tsp. ginger
1 tsp. vanilla

Crumble:
1 cup gluten-free oats
½ cup almond flour
½ cup slivered almonds
1 tsp. cinnamon
¼ tsp. ginger
½ tsp. sea salt
2 Tbsp. honey
2 Tbsp. coconut oil, melted
2–3 Tbsp. unsweetened almond milk

1. Spray crock with non-stick spray.

2. In the crock, combine nectarines, almonds, cinnamon, nutmeg, ginger, and vanilla.

3. In a medium bowl, combine all the crumble ingredients. If the mixture is too dry, add a bit more honey or almond milk. Pour over the top of the nectarine mixture.

4. Cover and cook on low for 2 hours.

Serving suggestion:

Serve over frozen vanilla Greek yogurt.

Calories: 210
Fat: 10g
Sodium: 80mg
Carbs: 24.5g
Sugar: 13g
Protein: 5g

- Gluten-Free
- Dairy-Free
- Vegetarian
- Soy-Free

- Low-Sodium
- Low-Cal
- Low-Fat

Blueberry Crinkle

Phyllis Good, Lancaster, PA

Makes 6–8 servings
Prep. Time: 15–20 minutes ⚜ Cooking Time: 2–3 hours ⚜ Ideal slow cooker size: 3- or 4-qt.

⅓ cup turbinado sugar
¾ cup gluten-free oats
½ cup gluten-free flour
½ tsp. cinnamon
dash of kosher salt
6 Tbsp. coconut oil, cold
4 cups blueberries, fresh or frozen
2 Tbsp. maple syrup
2 Tbsp. instant tapioca
2 Tbsp. lemon juice
½ tsp. lemon zest

1. Grease interior of slow cooker crock.

2. In a large bowl, combine turbinado sugar, oats, gluten-free flour, cinnamon, and salt.

3. Using two knives, a pastry cutter, or your fingers, work coconut oil into dry ingredients until small crumbs form.

4. In a separate bowl, stir together blueberries, maple syrup, tapioca, lemon juice, and lemon zest.

5. Spoon blueberry mixture into slow cooker crock.

6. Sprinkle crumbs over blueberries.

7. Cover. Cook 2–3 hours on low, or until firm in the middle with juice bubbling up around the edges.

8. Remove lid with a giant swoop away from yourself so condensation on inside of lid doesn't drip on the crumbs.

9. Lift crock out of cooker. Let cool until either warm or room temperature before eating.

Calories: 280
Fat: 12.5g
Sodium: 25mg
Carbs: 40.5g
Sugar: 21.5g
Protein: 2.8g

- Gluten-Free
- Dairy-Free
- Soy-Free
- Nut-Free

- Low-Sodium
- Vegetarian
- Low-Cal

Homestyle Bread Pudding

Lizzie Weaver, Ephrata, PA

Makes 6 servings

Prep. Time: 10–15 minutes & Cooking Time: 2–3 hours & Ideal slow cooker size: large enough to hold your baking insert

⅓ cup Egg Beaters

2¼ cups fat-free milk

½ tsp. ground cinnamon

¼ tsp. salt

⅓ cup maple syrup

1 tsp. vanilla

2 cups 1-inch bread cubes

½ cup raisins

1. Combine all ingredients in bowl. Pour into slow cooker baking insert. Cover baking insert. Place on metal rack (or rubber jar rings) in bottom of slow cooker.

2. Pour ½ cup hot water into cooker around outside of insert.

3. Cover slow cooker. Cook on high 2–3 hours.

4. Serve pudding warm or cold.

Calories: 150

Fat: .5g

Sodium: 230mg

Carbs: 32g

Sugar: 23g

Protein: 6g

- Vegetarian
- Nut-Free
- Low-Cal

- Low-Fat
- Low-Sodium

Fudgy Secret Brownies

Juanita Weaver, Johnsonville, IL

Makes 8 servings
Prep. Time: 10 minutes ⚬ Cooking Time: 1½–2 hours ⚬ Ideal slow cooker size: 6- or 7-qt.

4 oz. unsweetened chocolate

¾ cup coconut oil

¾ cup frozen diced okra, partially thawed

3 large eggs

1½ cups xylitol or your choice of sweetener

1 teaspoon pure vanilla extract

¼ tsp. mineral salt

¾ cup coconut flour

½–¾ cup coarsely chopped walnuts or pecans, optional

1. Melt chocolate and coconut oil in small saucepan.

2. Put okra and eggs in blender. Blend until smooth.

3. Measure all other ingredients in mixing bowl.

4. Pour melted chocolate and okra over the dry ingredients and stir with fork just until mixed.

5. Pour into greased slow cooker.

6. Cover and cook on high for 1½–2 hrs.

Calories: 450
Fat: 31.5g
Sodium: 130mg
Carbs: 35.5g
Sugar: 2g
Protein: 6.5g

- Gluten-Free
- Dairy-Free
- Vegetarian

- Soy-Free
- Low-Sodium
- Low-Sugar

Black Bean Brownies

Juanita Weaver, Johnsonville, IL

Makes 6–8 servings
Prep. Time: 5 minutes   ❧   Cooking Time: 1–1½ hours   ❧   Ideal slow cooker size: 5- or 6-qt.

15-oz. can of black beans, rinsed and drained

6 eggs

⅓ cup cocoa powder

1½ tsp. aluminum-free baking powder

½ tsp. baking soda

2 Tbsp. coconut oil

2 tsp. pure vanilla

⅓ cup Greek yogurt or cottage cheese

¾ cup xylitol or your choice of sweetener

¼ tsp. salt

1. Put all ingredients in a food processor or blender. Blend until smooth.

2. Pour into greased slow cooker.

3. Cover and cook for 1½ hours on high.

4. Cool in crock. For best taste, chill before serving.

Calories: 230
Fat: 8.5g
Sodium: 360mg
Carbs: 29g
Sugar: .5g
Protein: 11g

- Gluten-Free
- Vegetarian
- Low-Sugar
- Low-Sodium

- Low-Cal
- High-Protein
- Nut-Free
- Low-Fat

Zucchini Chocolate Chip Bars

Hope Comerford, Clinton Township, MI

Makes 8–10 servings
Prep Time: 10 minutes ⚜ Cooking Time: 2–3 hours ⚜ Cooling Time: 30 minutes ⚜
Ideal slow cooker size: 3-qt.

3 eggs

¾ cup turbinado sugar

1 cup all-natural applesauce

3 tsp. vanilla

3 cups whole wheat flour

1 tsp. baking soda

½ tsp. baking powder

2 tsp. cinnamon

¼ tsp. salt

2 cups peeled and grated zucchini

1 cup dark chocolate chips

1. Spray the crock with non-stick spray.

2. Mix together the eggs, sugar, applesauce, and vanilla.

3. In a separate bowl, mix together the flour, baking soda, baking powder, cinnamon, and salt. Add this to the wet mixture and stir just until everything is mixed well.

4. Stir in the zucchini and chocolate chips

5. Pour this mixture into the crock.

6. Cover and cook on low for 2–3 hours. Let it cool in crock for about 30 minutes, then flip it over onto a serving platter or plate. It should come right out.

Calories: 400
Fat: 12.5g
Sodium: 240mg
Carbs: 71.5g
Sugar: 34.5g
Protein: 7.5g

- Vegetarian
- Soy-Free
- Nut-Free

- Low-Sodium
- Low-Fat

Slow Cooker Tapioca

Nancy W. Huber, Green Park, PA

Makes 12 servings
Prep. Time: 10 minutes ⚜ Cooking Time: 3½ hours ⚜ Chilling Time: minimum 4 hours ⚜
Ideal slow cooker size: 4-qt.

2 quarts fat-free milk

I cup small pearl tapioca

½ cup honey

4 eggs, beaten

I tsp. vanilla

fruit of choice, optional

1. Combine milk, tapioca, and honey in slow cooker. Cook on high 3 hours.

2. Mix together eggs, vanilla, and a little hot milk from slow cooker. Add to slow cooker. Mix. Cook on high 20 more minutes.

3. Chill thoroughly, at least 4 hours. Serve with fruit.

Calories: 170
Fat: 1.5g
Sodium: 90mg
Carbs: 31g
Sugar: 20.5g
Protein: 7.5g

- Gluten-Free
- Vegetarian
- Soy-Free
- Low-Sodium
- Nut-Free
- Low-Cal
- Low-Fat

Coconut Rice Pudding

Hope Comerford, Clinton Township, MI

Makes 6 servings

Prep. Time: 5 minutes ⚜ *Cooking Time: 2½ hours* ⚜ *Ideal slow cooker size: 5- or 6-qt.*

2½ cups low-fat milk

14-oz. can light coconut milk

½ cup turbinado sugar

1 cup Arborio rice

1 stick cinnamon

1 cup dried cranberries, optional

1. Spray crock with non-stick spray.

2. In crock, whisk together the milk, coconut milk, and sugar.

3. Add in the rice and cinnamon stick.

4. Cover and cook on low about 2–2½ hours, or until rice is tender and the pudding has thickened.

5. Remove cinnamon sticks. If using cranberries, sprinkle on top of each bowl of Coconut Rice Pudding.

Calories: 250
Fat: 4g
Sodium: 70mg
Carbs: 48g
Sugar: 22g
Protein: 4g

- Gluten-Free
- Soy-Free
- Nut-Free

- Low-Cal
- Low-Fat
- Vegetarian

Dark Chocolate Peanut Butter Cocoa

Hope Comerford, Clinton Township, MI

Makes 10–12 servings

Prep Time: 5 minutes ⚬ Cook Time: 5–6 hours ⚬ Ideal slow cooker size: 3- or 4-qt.

8 cups almond milk

½ cup powdered peanut butter

¼ cup turbinado sugar

12 oz. dark chocolate, broken into pieces

1 Tbsp. vanilla

1. Combine almond milk, powdered peanut butter, and turbinado sugar in crock.

2. Cover and cook low for 5–6 hours.

3. Stir in chocolate and vanilla until chocolate is melted, then serve.

Calories: 260
Fat: 13g
Sodium: 220mg
Carbs: 30g
Sugar: 25g
Protein: 7g

- Gluten-Free
- Vegan
- Vegetarian
- Low-Sodium
- Soy-Free

Metric Equivalent Measurements

If you're accustomed to using metric measurements, I don't want you to be inconvenienced by the imperial measurements I use in this book.

Use this handy chart, too, to figure out the size of the slow cooker you'll need for each recipe.

Weight (Dry Ingredients)

1 oz		30 g
4 oz	¼ lb	120 g
8 oz	½ lb	240 g
12 oz	¾ lb	360 g
16 oz	1 lb	480 g
32 oz	2 lb	960 g

Slow Cooker Sizes

1-quart	0.96 l
2-quart	1.92 l
3-quart	2.88 l
4-quart	3.84 l
5-quart	4.80 l
6-quart	5.76 l
7-quart	6.72 l
8-quart	7.68 l

Volume (Liquid Ingredients)

½ tsp.		2 ml
1 tsp.		5 ml
1 Tbsp.	½ fl oz	15 ml
2 Tbsp.	1 fl oz	30 ml
¼ cup	2 fl oz	60 ml
⅓ cup	3 fl oz	80 ml
½ cup	4 fl oz	120 ml
⅔ cup	5 fl oz	160 ml
¾ cup	6 fl oz	180 ml
1 cup	8 fl oz	240 ml
1 pt	16 fl oz	480 ml
1 qt	32 fl oz	960 ml

Length

¼ in	6 mm
½ in	13 mm
¾ in	19 mm
1 in	25 mm
6 in	15 cm
12 in	30 cm

Special Diet Index

Special Diet Index   **325**

Recipe and Ingredient Index

About the Author

Hope Comerford is a mom, wife, elementary music teacher, blogger, recipe developer, public speaker, FitAddict Training fit leader, Young Living Essential Oils essential oil enthusiast/educator, and published author. In 2013, she was diagnosed with a severe gluten intolerance and since then has spent many hours creating easy, practical, and delicious gluten-free recipes that can be enjoyed by both those who are affected by gluten and those who are not.

Growing up, Hope spent many hours in the kitchen with her Meme (grandmother) and her love for cooking grew from there. While working on her master's degree when her daughter was young, Hope turned to her slow cookers for some salvation and sanity. It was from there she began truly experimenting with recipes and quickly learned she had the ability to get a little more creative in the kitchen and develop her own recipes.

In 2010, Hope started her blog, *A Busy Mom's Slow Cooker Adventures* to simply share the recipes she was making with her family and friends. She never imagined people all over the world would begin visiting her page and sharing her recipes with others as well. In 2013, Hope self-published her first cookbook *Slow Cooker Recipes: 10 Ingredients or Less and Gluten-Free* and then later wrote *The Gluten-Free Slow Cooker*.

Hope is thrilled to be working with Fix-It and Forget-It and representing such an iconic line of cookbooks. She is excited to bring her creativeness to the Fix-It and Forget-It brand. Her first Fix-It and Forget-It cookbook is *Fix-It and Forget-It Lazy & Slow Cookbook: 365 Days of Slow Cooker Recipes*.

Hope lives in the city of Clinton Township, Michigan near Metro Detroit. She's been a native of Michigan her whole life. She has been happily married to her husband and best friend, Justin, since 2008. Together they have two children, Ella and Gavin, who are her motivation, inspiration, and heart. In her spare time, Hope enjoys traveling, singing, cooking, reading books, spending time with friends and family, and relaxing.